Secret Service Chief

Secret

HARPER & BROTHERS · PUBLISHERS
NEW YORK

Service Chief

BY U. E. BAUGHMAN

with Leonard Wallace Robinson

To my wife and son, to my friends, and to my colleagues in the Secret Service, past and present, whose devotion to their country and to their Chief is unsurpassed, I dedicate this book. Without their full co-operation I could not have achieved my goals, and this book would not have been written.

U. E. BAUGHMAN

Contents

[vii]

CONTENTS

A section of illustrations follows page 164.

Foreword

DURING THE NEARLY THIRTEEN YEARS I WAS CHIEF of the United States Secret Service several persons suggested I share my experience with the rest of the world through a book. I rejected these suggestions for several reasons: not enough time to write a book—apprehension that I might, in some way, sound critical of a person in public office—or a feeling that I could not express myself in a way that would make interesting reading. But mainly I rejected the idea because my work and the goals I had set for myself and the Service had not been reached. Now I have retired. My work is finished. But the work and the responsibility of the United States Secret Service will go on.

A Wisp of Smoke and Other Dangers

A LARGE PORTION OF THE AMERICAN PEOPLE SAW the terrifying trickle of smoke before I did—on their television screens. It had started rising from the lectern while Cardinal Cushing of Boston gave the solemn invocation that always precedes the President's oath of office. I was standing right behind President Eisenhower and President-Elect Kennedy on the Inaugural platform, listening to the prayer.

Even in prayer a Secret Service agent is not allowed to bow his head when he is guarding the President of the United

States. So my gaze, at the moment the smoke started, was not downward but off into the crowd, away from the lectern. Suddenly something told me to look back toward it; perhaps a whiff of the smoke, perhaps a sudden murmur from the crowd below, perhaps some sixth sense. When I saw the actual smoke my heart, almost literally, seemed to stop.

Few know it to this day but those wisps of smoke could very easily have been the prelude to the worst disaster in the whole history of the United States. As Chief of the U.S. Secret Service, personally responsible for the safety of these two famous men in front of me, I knew quite certainly that a true holocaust was very possible at that moment.

The reasons why are simple: The Inaugural stand was made entirely of wood and was a potential tinderbox. It was attached to the Capitol Building, and the only entrance and exit to the stand was a single, four-foot-wide aisle which led into that building. On the crowded stand, as the Cardinal continued his prayer, were more than a hundred of the most prominent men and women of our times, the Presidents' wives and families, members of the Supreme Court, the Diplomatic Corps and Kennedy's Cabinet, the two Vice Presidents, ranking members of the both Houses, and other leaders in the arts, business and government. If there were a fire behind the smoke and it should spread quickly . . .

What my mind fixed on now as the possible source of fire was the forest of wires which lay underneath the stand. There were miles of them; radio, TV, recording, telephone and electrical wires. They were woven into the Inaugural stand; encircled it; bisected it; and they hung in great festoons from the underbelly of the structure to guarantee that America should see and hear this great spectacle in all its glorious detail. One huge interlocking complex came right up into the stand directly in front of the smoking lectern.

The Secret Service had had these wires checked and rechecked several times. Such precaution was a routine, and one that was thoroughly enforced. The last total going-over had been completed just ten minutes before the stand had started to fill, and when each and every wire had passed final muster we had posted guards around to see that no unauthorized person should tamper with them.

Still, with all our care, something had gone awry. I knew at once from the kind and quality of the smoke that the trouble was a short circuit. The important questions were, of course, where was it and could we find it in time to prevent a conflagration?

My thoughts were a good deal swifter than it takes to tell, and within a second after first seeing the smoke I motioned to one of the Secret Service agents stationed near the lectern to summon the firemen we had posted throughout the stand in case of just such an eventuality. He did so and a fireman immediately went down to the lectern with a hand extinguisher. Meanwhile another agent was instructed to summon men to look for the short circuit. A feverish search ensued.

My first impulse was to clear the Inaugural stand forthwith. Three times I started to give that order and three times I resisted that impulse. The thing that made me hesitate was the possibility of panic. Everybody on the stand would have to get through that single door into the Capitol Building and if there were any tendency to stampede there could be a disaster. On the other hand I had to weigh that possibility against

[3]

the far graver disaster that would occur if an uncontrollable fire broke out in the stand.

As long as the smoke ascended from the lectern my tension was almost unendurable. Mainly, I suppose, because I was forcing myself *not* to take action. But finally, after an eternity of four minutes, the smoke suddenly stopped. By great good fortune, the kind you have when you actually find the needle in the haystack, the short-circuiting wires were located by one of the firemen and disconnected from their source of power. The smoldering died down immediately and the Inauguration proceeded on schedule.

I felt suddenly exhausted after the danger was over, wrung out, even more so than I normally would be after this kind of a crisis. Such fare, such excitements were regular features of my daily life. I remember noting this sudden exhaustion and thinking momentarily that perhaps I was getting too old after thirty-three years in the Secret Service. Perhaps its moment-to-moment alarums and excursions, the heavy, heavy responsibility of maintaining the safety of the President and his family twenty-four hours a day—perhaps these were getting too much for me. But then again, I thought, it probably is merely the cumulative effect of more recent pressures, those that occur between every election night and every inauguration. As Chief of the Secret Service I got those pressures directly.

This interregnum between Senator Kennedy's election and his inauguration had been chock-full of difficulties and problems. They started on election night. By law we had to continue giving full Secret Service protection to President Eisenhower as long as he was in office. But also, by law, I had to maintain full protection for the President-elect and his family from the very second it became clear he'd won the election. But would the winner be Nixon or Kennedy?

By election night the two candidates were a continent apart. Mr. Nixon on the West Coast and Senator Kennedy at his home in Hyannis Port on Cape Cod. This meant I had to dispatch a full complement of my top Secret Service agents to both candidates. On either coast these two hand-picked bands, fifteen in each, waited impatiently in the wings.

We are not allowed to give candidates personal protection before election results are in. So the two Secret Service units had to stay on the alert in quarters as close to Vice President Nixon and Senator Kennedy as they could get. I stayed glued to my television set at home, with direct telephonic communication set up with both camps. If the election had been "normal" I could have let them know what to do by midnight, protect their man or hasten back for further duties.

But the night and the suspense dragged on till dawn and after. Finally at 6 A.M. I just made up my mind on my own and picked up my direct line to the Holiday Hearth Motel in West Yarmouth, Massachusetts, four miles from Hyannis Port, where my men were stationed. "Take over the protection of President-Elect Kennedy at once," I told Inspector Burrill Peterson, who was in charge of this advance group.

It was a precarious decision to make before California and Illinois and some of the other states were certain—and before many of the pundits had made up their minds who'd won. But I hated to see the probable winner go without protection a moment longer, and so I took a chance. If I'd been wrong I don't know what the consequences would have been, but I am sure the other candidate would have been furious at me and I guess I wouldn't have blamed him. Actually there's only one way to avoid putting the Secret Service in such an untenable position. It is to allow us by law to give full protection to *both* candidates from election-day midnight on till it's absolutely certain who has been elected. Then nobody will have his feelings hurt.

There were many, many funny and interesting things that happened as soon as we started protecting the Kennedys and I will come to them in time. For the moment I am only going to tell the unknown facts about a few typical events that happened backstage in the lives of the new First Family. These will give the first inkling of the important and varied events the Secret Service is called upon to handle—and perhaps may indicate why my tension of the first few months preceding the Inauguration had been cumulative.

There were many crises with the Kennedys but the first to develop fully proceeded from the new First Lady's pregnancy. After returning from Hyannis Port Mrs. Kennedy had taken up residence at their house on N Street in Georgetown, a residential section of Washington. Senator Kennedy badly needed a rest after the election and it was decided that he would go to Palm Beach from Hyannis Port for a vacation and that Mrs. Kennedy would join him later.

The President-elect returned from Palm Beach for Thanksgiving and was about to land when he received news of an urgent call awaiting him. Mrs. Kennedy had started to give birth two months before the child was due.

Here's how it all happened. I had stationed a very carefully selected group of agents to protect Mrs. Kennedy. And, as was our custom with a First Family, I had assigned hand-picked men to guard Caroline. Suddenly, without warning, Mrs. Kennedy informed a member of the White House staff that she had better get to the hospital quickly. She thought she was about to have her baby.

The Secret Service had foreseen this possibility and we were fully prepared for it. The hospital (Georgetown) had been decided on beforehand by the Presidential couple and their choice had been made known to us. We had laid out a careful route to this hospital which would avoid all traffic and get Mrs. Kennedy there as quickly as possible. Also, we had obtained the name of Mrs. Kennedy's obstetrician and a schedule of his whereabouts twenty-four hours a day. And we had a special car ready at all times just in case the birth should happen to be premature. Such prescience was routine for us; it was the way we always thought.

Our preparations paid off. Everything went off with absolute precision. The doctor was summoned to the hospital in time and performed a successful Caesarian operation, and John Fitzgerald Kennedy, Jr., was born safely and immediately put in a special care unit.

And then a nasty event happened.

As Mrs. Kennedy was being wheeled back from the delivery room after her operation a man suddenly stepped out from a concealed position. He had an expensive camera with a flashbulb on it. The new First Lady was still unconscious from the anesthetic, but as far as this miserable creature was concerned this was all the better—his picture would be that much more valuable. He took her photograph as she lay there.

He did not have long to gloat over his idiotic triumph. We

teach the agents to be infinitely patient and forbearing with the public and many of them have faced death (as you will discover) without drawing their firearms if that seems the course of action safest for the President or his family. But this provocation was too much. The agents I had put in charge of Mrs. Kennedy had been walking well behind the stretcher; they saw instantly what had happened and came up swiftly. When the stretcher had passed, one of them took the camera from the man's hand and, in a very unforbearing way, ripped the film out of it. Then the other collared the fellow and with infinite lack of patience led him off.

Upsetting and distasteful as this incident was, it was only a prelude to something that might have actually taken the life of the new-born Kennedy infant and the other babies in his ward.

The young fellow (who, incidentally, looked exactly like his father from the moment he was born, with a great shock of hair on the top of his head) was kept in an incubator in the premature baby room. Generally several of the babies in this room are receiving oxygen and this life-sustaining gas is highly inflammable. Smoking or lighting a cigarette is strictly forbidden of course. There is no question but that an exploding flashbulb could cause an explosion or a flash fire that might be disastrous.

Such possibilities did not deter certain photographers. Scouting around to get their pictures they found that, while the nurses on the premature ward were dedicated and incorruptible, there were certain X-ray technicians who were allowed to go into the ward on special occasions.

One of these X-ray technicians was approached and offered

three hundred dollars to get a picture of the baby. By pure luck the technician who was thus tempted told one of the nurses about the offer. This nurse told the authorities at once and we closed off the entire area to everybody except nurses and doctors during the entire time that the Kennedy mother and child were at the hospital.

Incidents like these give one a preliminary view of just why we of the Secret Service have come to believe that our Presidents and their families are, potentially, in permanent danger, often from totally unexpected quarters. And it is why we believe they need the most constant and expert protection, day and night. Even so, the experiences above are relatively mild examples compared with the dangers President Eisenhower and President Truman faced and survived during their terms of office and I will go into detail about these dangers when I come to describe the various techniques and devices the Secret Service uses to keep our Presidents safe.

One preinaugural experience Senator Kennedy had, however, ranks with the closest calls any President ever had. I believe few know the real facts and hardly anybody realized just how near we came one bright December morning to losing our President-elect to a madman.

This insane individual was one Richard P. Pavlick. At 9:50 A.M. on Sunday, December 11, 1960, according to his own statement, Pavlick was parked in his car on the street directly in front of the Kennedy residence in Palm Beach, Florida. In his car were seven sticks of dynamite all rigged up and ready to be detonated by a jerk of his hand on a switch. Pavlick was waiting for the President-elect to come out of his home to go to Sunday mass. Senator Kennedy's car was parked directly in front of his residence and was of course surrounded by his Secret Service contingent. The would-be assassin fully intended to drive his own car from its parking place the moment he saw the President-elect enter his car. His plan was to smash into the Kennedy car and, at the moment of impact, pull the knife switch that would detonate the dynamite. There was enough dynamite to blow up a small mountain and, unquestionably, it would have wiped out Senator Kennedy, Pavlick and all the Secret Service agents, as well as anybody else anywhere near by.

Pavlick was completely prepared to give up his own life in this attempt. By rare good fortune when President-Elect Kennedy came out of his house Mrs. Kennedy, with the children, had come to the door to say good-by to him. Some spark of humanity revived in Pavlick. "I did not wish to harm her or the children," he told us later. "I decided to get him at the church or someplace later."

The Secret Service of course had no inkling of the fact that Pavlick was in Florida. However, we were actually on his trail at that moment. Just two days before we had received information from a Post Office Inspector in Belmont, New Hampshire, that a local character, probably insane, had uttered threats against the life of the President-elect. The man's name was Pavlick. We made a routine check at that point but it was not until the fourteenth of December that we found that Pavlick was probably on his way to Palm Beach. Of course we immediately started an all-out search and were able to take him into custody within twenty-four hours.

The closeness of the call was appalling. And the more I reviewed the details of the case, the worse it became.

Pavlick, it developed, had not just been a madman with a random impulse. He had planned the assassination with care. He had taken pictures of Senator Kennedy's home, and of the church he attended, in order to study them carefully. After his last-minute abandonment of his plan outside the Kennedy home Pavlick had decided to kill the President-elect in or near the church. He had gone to this church several times to study the layout and was there at least once when the President-elect was inside!

The miasma of madness hangs about all this man's statements and all the things he had committed to paper.

A letter was found on him which read in part: "I believe that the Kennedys bought the Presidency and the Whitehouse and until he really became President it was my intention to remove him in the only way it was available to me; the Supreme Court wouldn't enter any motion of mine, if asked, to stop the oath of office."

Many an insane, would-be assassin writes a letter addressed to the "People of the United States" and has it upon him when he makes his homicidal attempt. Such a document, according to Secret Service experience, usually means that the individual is ultimately dangerous and has every intention of going through with his plan. One was found on Pavlick, rambling and incoherent, but clear always about his murderous intent. Its contents assumed that the dreadful act, the murder of President-Elect Kennedy by dynamite, had already been completed, and read, in part:

If death and destruction and injury to persons has resulted from my vicious action then I am truly sorry, but it won't help any. It is hoped that by my actions that a better country and a more attentive citizenry has resulted and corrected any abuses of ambitious moneyed persons or groups, then it will not have been in vain. . . . It was unfortunate for the Kennedy's that John was elected president because it was Jimmy Hoffa who was to have been my target of destruction because of his "Go to hell the United States" attitude and because of the gutless cowards called The Congress of the United States who are afraid to clip his wings. . . .

Pavlick, the photographers in the hospital, and now the smoking wires in the lectern—such were the characteristic crises following Senator Kennedy's election. Surely the Secret Service was in for a lively era protecting this brisk, handsome, athletic and physically fearless man. These were my thoughts as the Inauguration ceremonies, when the smoking of the lectern had subsided, proceeded without further hitch or danger.

Well, my retrospective thoughts continued, you weathered far more than these adventures before you came to Washington and since. And my mind went back and back to beginnings, to earlier crises, the crucible of experiences, some funny, some sad, some frightening—the ones that make and shape a man. At the beginning these experiences had mostly concerned the pursuit of counterfeiters—and other criminals who were a threat to our currency. The duties of the Secret Service included the protection of our money as well as our President.

Cops and Robbers

MAINLY, IN THESE PAGES, I AM GOING TO TELL MY experiences as Chief of the U.S. Secret Service. But these will be more intelligible if I tell something first of my past life.

I can be pretty brief about a good deal of it—the first twenty-seven years anyhow. They can be summarized by recounting an incident that occurred outside the Lyric Theater in Camden, New Jersey, one warm night in June, 1932. I had never felt *real* fear up to that time and the experience of it was profoundly disturbing and proved a turning point in my whole outlook, particularly in my attitude toward being a Secret Service man.

It was 9:30 in the evening and I was waiting outside the

theater for two "mad-dog" extortionists to show their hand. As per their instructions I had a newspaper tucked under my left arm and I held a cardboard box in my right hand. The box was supposed to contain five thousand dollars in small bills. Actually it held neat stacks of white bond paper, the size, shape and weight of our national currency but with no further resemblance to it.

I had been in the Secret Service for five years by that time and had just passed my twenty-seventh birthday. The evening's experience (as had been all of my experiences in the Service up till then) I fully expected to be a high-spirited, exciting episode, a kind of cops-and-robbers adventure. It turned out, however, to be a personal nightmare.

The whole thing had begun when George W. Norris, Governor of the Federal Reserve Bank of Philadelphia, had received an extortion note, demanding five thousand dollars for "protection." If he did not turn over the money, the note ominously stated, he would "suffer." He was told to signify his intention of complying with the demand by inserting an ad in the Personals Column of the Philadelphia *Inquirer*.

Governor Norris referred the matter to William H. Houghton, who then headed the Philadelphia office of the Secret Service. From then on Bill Houghton carried the ball in this matter. He inserted the ad in the newspaper and when he received further instructions, telling us to have an intermediary at the Lyric movie house with the money, he picked me for the job.

Bill Houghton was a wonderful man and I shall never forget him. It was under him that, in many ways, I grew up, both professionally and personally in the Secret Service. When he selected me for this important and dangerous mission I was enormously proud. Had I known his motives, learned many years later, I would not have been so puffed up at that exact moment. After I became Chief I once visited with him in Philadelphia and the subject of the Norris extortion case came up. "Why did you pick me for that job?" I asked him then. "Did you really think I was that good?"

He laughed. "Not at that point," he said. "But I had to give you a chance to realize that this was a serious business, not just a game of cops and robbers. And you *were* promising."

The realization did indeed strike me that night. As I stood there under the lonely illumination of a small city movie marquee my buoyancy gradually began to leave me. After 9:30 passers-by were few in Camden, New Jersey, in the depression year of 1932.

The minutes began to tick by: 9:35 . . . 9:40 . . . 9:45 . . . For almost ten minutes nobody passed. It was now 9:55, and then, from the distance, I heard the slow measured click of a pair of leather heels. This would be the man (we didn't know at the time there were two of them). I waited almost eagerly to have the thing over with. A laboring man in overalls clacked by without looking at me.

Another five minutes passed. It was the waiting, of course, that finally got me. I began to feel increasingly and inexplicably anxious. I'd never had this feeling before. My skin and scalp began to prickle. I felt like the bull's-eye of a target peered at down a gun barrel; totally vulnerable. Actually I was the focus of a small army of Secret Service men who had me under surveillance as part of Bill Houghton's plan. They

[15]

watched from doorways, rooftops and a parked car across the street, their tommy guns and pistols ready. . . .

And now my imagination began really to run riot. The extortionist was clearly a desperate man or he would not have run such risks. What if he drove up and insisted I come with him at gun point? If I went he'd discover the fake money and, out of sheer frustration, would probably kill me. If, on the other hand, I resisted, he'd probably kill me anyhow. And if, as was probable, my circle of protectors should decide to save me, there'd be a gun battle of course, with me at the dead center of that steel-slinging arc of protectors and the bullets would funnel toward me. . . .

Thirty minutes had gone by. Now, perhaps in defense against the intimations of panic I felt, recollections from my past began to confront me—exactly as one reads about it in books when a character is in danger. Details, some isolated and meaningless, some apparently connected with my present plight, floated into my mind.

I thought of the games of cops and robbers we used to play endlessly when I was a boy. I used to love that game. Oddly, I used to like the part of a robber better than that of one of the cops. I prided myself on my craftiness in the places I picked to hide, and on my patience and my stillness within my hiding place. I felt crafty, primitive, infinitely cunning. Once I hid up in a tree, lying out on one of the branches just above my pursuers, concealed by the leaves—I lay there for hours on that narrow branch, unmoving, until finally the "cops" had to give up. And even then I did not come down. I stayed on for another half-hour or so, to "test" my endurance. I wonder why, even now. At fifteen, when baseball and football com-

manded most of my attention, I still had a sneaking passion
for cops and robbers and once played it with some younger
boys with all the old passion, though I felt a bit guilty at playing such a "kids' " game.

Fifteen: that was the year my father became ill and the
year I realized what a brave man he was. He'd been a successful contractor and had been taken ill on the job—he'd
had a stroke and from then on was partially paralyzed. Yet as
soon as he was able, he'd insisted on figuring out something
he could do to support us. He had opened a dry-goods store
with his small savings and, with my dear mother's help, he
hoped we'd get by. We did, too, on his raw courage; our
money dwindled slowly and I couldn't go to college, but he
kept the family, myself and my mother and my two sisters,
together.

Courage. I wasn't showing much of it now as I waited. I
looked up and down the street. Nobody. The thought of my
father had made me feel a little better. He never quit on anything. He was a strong man, a good man, the head of his
house, and no doubt about that. I disappointed him once, I
remembered.

He'd wanted me to go into business. I'd gotten a job as a
salesman with a company that sold coal stoves, just to please
him. I was nineteen years old. I hated that job. I was terrible
at selling and I felt lonely and miserable in the hotel rooms of
the small towns that I had to travel through.

I was sent forth by my mentor, a Mr. Shellabarger, owner
of the stove company, with a whole hatful of practical advice,
ranging from the way to smile to the details of my sales
pitches. I went on a prearranged schedule through the small

towns and cities of New England. I received a letter from
Mr. Shellabarger almost daily. Yet I sold no stoves in Paw-
tucket or Providence, Rhode Island, or Dedham, Needham,
Boston or Worcester, Massachusetts. I kept on, however, and
at last the miracle happened; to my undying astonishment a
hardware merchant in a small town in Connecticut bought
one of my stoves. I hastened to get the order off to Mr. Shellabarger. In my letter to him I mentioned the fact that I did
not like the town and I could not wait for the only train of
the day, which would appear at 5 P.M., to take me out of it.
His letter, sent to New Haven, my next stop, came whizzing
back at me. I have preserved it to this day, for, in my young
and yeasty condition, it proved to be the *coup de grâce* to my
career in the marketplace. It read:

DEAR URBANUS [*sic*; that is my real first name—it took a Mr.
Shellabarger to salute me with it]:
Yours from Connecticut received. We congratulate you on your
initial order. The Modern Age Hardware Company to whom you
sold that stove has a fair credit rating. We'll wait and see. Now in
referring to what you said about getting out of that small town
fast; one thing I omitted to caution you about, was not to be
governed by time tables. Take time to complete your business, it
is better to stay a few extra hours than to hasten away for a train.
The dollar is more important than your feelings. Please do not
offer five per cent for cash. Will write tomorrow to either Hart-
ford or New London.

As I stood outside the Lyric Theater in Camden I could
feel the same appalling aloneness I had felt when I was on
the road for Mr. Shellabarger, particularly when darkness
came on; a feeling now mingled with fear. It was thirty-five
minutes I'd been standing there and no one had appeared. I

looked toward one of the Secret Service men parked in the car across the street. He gave me the prearranged signal to hold my position. I leaned back against the building. . . .

Mr. Shellabarger's letter finished me. I quit and went home by the next train. I decided that business wasn't for me—and for the next three years I rattled around. I went to business school at night; took typing; did odd jobs; went to college at night, the University of Pennsylvania. Then I heard about the Secret Service and I applied at the Philadelphia office and I was accepted. From the very first day I loved it. It seemed the answer to some of my deepest needs.

The atmosphere at the Philadelphia branch of the Secret Service seemed charged with excitement on that first day, as if the whole organization were engaged in a gigantic game of cops and robbers and as if the enchantment of my child-hood had returned. The very air seemed electrified—agents came and went, absorbed in thought; one was stuffing a brief case ready to depart on a dangerous mission; clerks with sleeves rolled up bent over clacking typewriters. All was action and tension.

I started as a clerk and right from the beginning no two days were alike for me. My notebooks were stuffed with dictation —agents' reports, verbatim statements from suspects. And then, gradually, I was initiated into other tasks. I was sent to pick up counterfeit notes from a bank when they appeared, for the Secret Service was called at once when a counterfeit reached a bank. And I was taught to maintain the office files on cases, to search and to extract the important elements from the records of the criminals we had to deal with.

I was made to study the history of the Secret Service too,

to learn its traditions, its glories and achievements, its nationwide duties, the instructive experiences of its agents in the past. The government had launched the organization in 1865 in response to a wave of counterfeiting that had nearly inundated our currency and pursuing the counterfeiter had been one of its chief activities ever since. But in 1901 after President McKinley had been assassinated by the insane Polish worker, Leon Czolgosz, Congress had added the protection of the President to our duties. None too soon either, for this was our third President to be killed by madmen who should have been in mental institutions. None has been killed since, though there have been some close calls.

Protecting the President, of course, became one of our most urgent tasks through the years and the techniques we worked out made us known for this function alone. But gradually we took over other duties too; the pursuit of government check forgers; the pursuit of government bond thieves; the protection of the United States Treasury against theft; in short, all crimes directed against our currency became, eventually, the responsibility of the Secret Service.

Naturally our agents through the years had had tremendous adventures and I loved studying about them. They fed my dreams.

Then, finally, the real glory descended upon me. This happened when I discovered that real, live agents in the here and now would be willing to let me accompany them at night on their investigations. This was the essence of glamour. Now I came into actual contact with actual criminals, just as if I were an agent myself, not a lowly clerk. The excitement of these nightly forays into Philadelphia's Tenderloin and other sections of the city where counterfeiters hung out was almost too much for me sometimes. How right I had been to hate selling stoves. *This* was living. . . .

Suddenly the marquee lights on the Lyric went out and, as if by signal, a car pulled up in front of the movie house. I could make out two figures, one in the driver's seat and one next to him. Why were they sitting there? Was a gun trained on me? I wanted to run, to hide. I wanted to duck behind the cashier's booth. I really had to fight myself to keep from reaching down and feeling my gun. Cold sweat broke out on my forehead. Would the bullets from my "protectors" start funneling toward me soon; *what* were the two waiting for?

They were obviously casing the situation. It took them about five minutes to do so and then slowly they drove off. As I saw them go I was dreadfully relieved. They had decided that the whole thing was too risky. When their tail light could no longer be seen I started to go across the street and suddenly I saw that the agent in the car was beckoning me angrily to return to my post. I obeyed.

And now another wait again; but this time for not so long. In six or seven minutes a boy of about twelve came along the street. "Mister," he said, "have you got a cardboard box you were supposed to give to somebody?"

"Yes," I said. I handed him the package and asked, trying not to move my lips, "Who sent you and where are they?"

He was a bright, alert boy. "Two men asked me to do it for them. In a car."

"Where are they?" I asked again.

"Down two blocks and around the corner," he said.

"Okay," I said, "you give them the box and then walk away fast."

He looked scared at my words but he did as I told him. I walked across the street as casually as possible and when I got within speaking distance of the agents' car I said: "Acorn Street to the right. The boy was sent by them."

The four agents were out of their car in the twinkling of an eye. The five of us moved over to the side of the street the Lyric was on and followed the path the little boy had taken. We moved softly but swiftly.

Our timing was perfect. The youngster had just given the criminals the "loot" and left. A warning bullet from one of our guns and the two extortioners gave up. They were not the steely type; but they could have been dangerous if given a chance for they were armed to the teeth: two pistols each and a submachine gun, fully loaded and ready to fire.

Scared as I'd been in front of the movie house, I hadn't shaken. Now, in the aftermath, I trembled like a leaf. Perhaps none of the agents noticed; if they did they said nothing. Doubtless they had had the same reactions themselves.

The Philadelphia papers got hold of the story and splashed it all over the front pages. For my role I was a sort of hero, according to the accounts. I knew better myself. I knew what my own feelings had been.

I grew up that night. Never again was I to look upon the pursuit of the criminal as if it were a game to be played for my personal delight. It was deadly serious, this business of being a policeman. It took courage and it took conviction. It was a life-or-death matter, for myself and for the man I was pursuing. Each of us, the criminal and I, was a human being, with every form of human emotion, terror, love, fear; our relationship was essentially a tragic one. Only men who took this view, I now realized, deserved to be called policemen.

Bill Houghton sensed (he later told me) that I had turned a corner that night in Camden and now he began to pile "experience" on me in earnest. In the next twenty-four months he threw everything my way.

In those days protecting our currency meant almost exclusively the pursuit and capture of the counterfeiter. It was, then, to this branch of the work that Mr. Houghton now directed my energies exclusively.

I became an expert at "roping." This is the Secret Service technique in which we pass ourselves off in the underworld as criminals; when we succeed in doing this, we can then work our way into a known counterfeiter's confidence, our object being to get him to sell his contraband to us. If we can get him to do this, then we have him, legally speaking, very literally roped. "Roping" is a hard and dangerous business, one of the stocks-in-trade of the Secret Service, with many twists and turns that one must learn. The Secret Service brought it, during those years, to a high degree of perfection and later I was to formulate the techniques we developed into an entire course that every Secret Service man is now required to take. I also learned the arduous and tricky business of shadowing, of collecting the difficult kinds of evidence necessary to convict a counterfeiter, the techniques of raiding. The details of these various skills are as fascinating to read about as the lore of any big game hunter, and these too I later formulated into courses for my men.

By 1934 I was handling over two hundred cases of every type annually. It would require another book to tell of the adventures and narrow escapes I had. Flipping the years like pages I see many interesting and instructive highlights—and some funny ones too.

There was the time I made my first arrest. Bill Houghton sent me alone to take in a small-time passer of counterfeit named Joe Huchner who lived in a cheap rooming house in a run-down section of Philadelphia. On the way I worked myself into a highly serious, limb-of-the-law frame of mind. I knocked on the suspect's door authoritatively, gun in hand, careful to keep my body screened by the wall.

"Come in," he called out.

"You're under arrest," I said, peering through the door, my gun pointing at him.

"Oh, really?" he said casually. "Well, I'll be with you in a moment." He was in his bathrobe, smoking. "Won't you come in," he said. I entered warily. "I really won't take a second," he said. "Please sit down."

I was nonplused, literally disarmed, for I even put away my gun. Then I sat down. He did dress quickly too, but while he did so he told me two terribly funny jokes, and I recall laughing long and hard at them. I suppose I was relieved to have the tension of my first "pinch" reduced to such a low pitch. But that's the only excuse I'll try to give. By the time we got to HQ I had developed some peculiarly friendly feelings toward this "charming" hood.

These changed abruptly in the next few minutes, however.

"Where's the counterfeit?" Houghton asked me after I booked my prize.

"Huh?" I asked. I looked blank indeed. I flushed. I'd completely forgotten to search my hood's room. His airy manner and social graces had made me forget the performance of my routine duties completely. Bill Houghton gave me a withering look, but he said no more. Older men than I had been taken in by the Huchner charms.

I learned my lesson. Crooks can be terribly ingratiating people at times; even the really tough ones can have a curious quality of likableness about them. I have been careful to be on particular guard against such personal charm, real or counterfeit, ever since my experience with Joe Huchner.

But you not only had to develop resistance to a crook's charm. In the long, arduous business of roping criminals by passing as one of them you had to put down, ruthlessly, any feelings of friendship that might develop. Your game was to win their confidence so they would, finally, trust you.

To this end you had to act a part that would arouse feelings of admiration and respect in a felon's breast. If he was tough, you had to be tougher; if he had served time, you'd served twice as much; if he drove a hard bargain over the price for his counterfeit, you had to make David Harum look like a gullible amateur. In the end you came to dwell, like Abraham, in the criminal's bosom, for by this time, you had become his ideal, a lawbreaker with greater scorn for society, tougher and harder than he was. His awakening was to be rude indeed.

Often I dreaded the hour when the showdown came. For it was impossible, in the dangerous intimacy that had developed over days and weeks, not to have felt the humanness of the other person; to have learned his hopes and fears and even his loves; to have been privileged also to glimpse the terrible rage

[25]

toward society he felt and his expectation of nothing but betrayal from it. And when the moment came for the cycle of his betrayal to come full turn and to see him at that moment as vulnerable as a child, his incredulous gaze turning on you with full knowledge of your betrayal of him dawning slowly and painfully upon his face—well, those moments were very, very hard to take.

When they occurred I had to remember that I was not society's judge but its police officer—that morally, no act was all black or white but that every act must be judged in shades of gray. And that I must do my duty whatever my feelings.

At such moments I had to force myself to remember hard what the criminal might have done to me had he caught me first. I had such an example I could always keep green in my memory.

It was 11 P.M., December 12, 1934. I was with Domenico and Vincent Donatoni in a restaurant in Philadelphia. These two men were large-scale passers of counterfeit money, whom I had completely persuaded that I was a big-time mobster from the Coast. I had, with due subtlety, insisted that, before I made a purchase from them, I must meet their boss. They had, at length, agreed.

The "Boss" arrived five or ten minutes late with a good-looking blonde in tow. I recognized her at once. She had been the girl friend of a counterfeiter I had arrested two years before, a small-time gangster named Sam Carter. She had been with him when I arrested him and though she had not seen me for long, perhaps five minutes in a poorly lighted room, her face now registered the shock of recognition.

"That ain't one of us," she said at once, pointing right at me. "That's a copper. I know him. He put the arm on Sammy. His name is Brennan or somethin'."

Luckily, I was able to cover my highly justified agitation. I looked at her incredulously, as though she were some unspeakably distasteful thing the wind had blown in or the sea had turned up, and said, "Who's this crazy dame?"

Her boy friend's eyes bulged with suspicion, of course. He put his hand inside his coat and turned to the Donatoni boys, his face an ugly question mark.

I'd done a good job. "It's impossible," they said. "His name is Harry Warren. He's from Los Angeles. Tommy Ryan himself okayed him. He's been in stir with Tommy. He's a big man himself." Tommy Ryan had indeed okayed me. He was a small-time gangster who'd fallen on hard times in the underworld and had turned to informing.

The Donatonis listed my criminal pedigree, while I looked on disgustedly at the whole proceeding.

When they had finished the blonde looked ever so slightly less sure of herself. "Whaddaya think?" her boy friend asked.

She shook her head. "Maybe I'm wrong," she said. "But he sure looks like that guy to me."

Their boss turned to the Donatonis. "Get Tommy Ryan over here," he said.

Domenico took off and we all sat down in silence, the boss scrutinizing me balefully. In the hour we waited for Domenico to return he allowed himself only one remark. "You better be Harry Warren, Mac," he said. "If you ain't him I ain't gonna kill you fast at all."

[27]

I allowed myself a reply; looking at the blonde I put on a look compounded of five parts boredom and three parts condensed malignancy and said: "Dumb ——— broad."

Inside, however, I didn't feel at all bored. Would Tommy Ryan stick to his guns as an informer? He might figure that nobody would know if he fingered me. And it would put him in solid with this group if he did. Also, if they finally found out that I really was a cop, and a Federal one at that, Tommy's life wouldn't be worth a nickel.

Anyhow, when he arrived he looked at me in consternation. "What's this?" he said. "That's Harry Warren. That ain't no copper. He's a hunnerd per cent."

They could have killed the blonde but she just shrugged and said: "So I made a mistake. So sue me."

I backed out of the case fast after that night so that Tommy Ryan wouldn't get into serious underworld trouble when we arrested this gang. And we did arrest them soon enough, including the blonde, as an accessory after the fact. I am happy to say that the charges against her stuck, and I am not normally a vindictive man.

I worked on over two thousand counterfeiting cases before I became Chief. I have had to play every kind of criminal role from a hobo to a smooth international operator. Some of the cases that came my way were big ones, some small. One I always remember was the one in which I played the role of a bindlestiff.

The counterfeiters in that case were a small gang of hobos who were turning out a really excellent brand of half-dollar. To rope them I had to dress as a hobo myself and go after them in their natural habitat, the hobo jungle. I found them living on the edge of a small stream next to a cornfield, and they welcomed me into their midst without a question. I ate and slept with them for a week and learned to like their debonair spirit and sense of fun.

Those were the depression years and many good men were footloose, unable to get jobs or to keep body and soul together. These men were of that kind. Despite the hard times they had fallen upon I shall always remember them and the way in which they kept their love of life alive.

Their little magic half-dollar stamping machine was hidden in the cornfield. It was a simple device with a very good die made by an unemployed engraver in the gang—and one of the others, an unemployed metallurgist, had made a particularly deceptive amalgam of metals that, shaped into a coin, looked and felt quite real and sounded so too if dropped upon a counter.

Whenever this hardy little band would run out of their modest necessities they would repair to their cornfield and have a manufacturing session, never making more coins than they needed. When I, at last, had to stop them the newspapers had great fun with them, calling them the Cornfield Counterfeiters and me the Cornfield Cop. I am happy to say that this happy group got off with a stern warning from an understanding judge; happy, that is, because they were not basically criminals but men who were trying merely to keep body, soul and good spirits together in an era of genuine hardship.

Sometimes I had as many as three "roping" cases going at one time. At such junctures the problem was to keep my identities straight to myself; my various names, backgrounds, peculiarities. I could have trapped myself easily if my memory had failed me. Or if one of the crooks I was after had, by chance, happened to know the other.

Big cases came my way, too. Some of them made the boldest kinds of headlines at the time. The names of most of these criminals have been forgotten, even by myself. Some, however, are still memorable, immortalized by the shame or horror of their acts. For an example of the latter kind; I pursued and caught the arch-criminal Herman Petrillo, head of Murder, Inc. The work I did on this case led directly to the exposure of his fiendish murder-for-insurance syndicate. This monster is always mentioned as one of the worst criminals of all time and my part in putting him away did not hurt my reputation.

Indeed, there were occasionally some small indications that they knew at least my name in Washington. And while this might have been of merely academic interest to me up till 1936, after that time it became of increasing practical importance. For in that year I fell in love with a Miss Ruth Yessel, and though I was not exactly the whirlwind type with the ladies in general, I was in her book and we were married on August 5 of that year. At first we made out all right on my salary but then Bill was born and, just in the nick of time, financially speaking, Washington smiled on my endeavors. The powers that be made me Assistant to the Supervising Agent in New York City.

It was a big jump for me. The Secret Service has fifty-nine regional offices in the United States and these handle the hundreds of counterfeiting and check-forging cases that occur in this country annually. But New York was and is the hottest of all the regional offices and I really liked it there, for I loved my work and in New York the cases came thicker and faster and more interesting than ever.

Too, I had a chance to get some administrative experience and to learn a bit about the techniques of protecting visiting dignitaries and occasionally even members of the President's family when they came to town.

And so it went till, in the course of time, I was myself made top dog in New York. For my money that meant I'd reached the zenith—that was as far as a man could go. Or should decently want to. Supervising Agent of the New York area. What could even be imagined as more desirable? We settled in, then, Ruth and Bill and I, to enjoying life at the top.

And then the phone call came.

chapter **3**

The Reluctant Chief

I REMEMBER WITH ABSOLUTE CLARITY THE DE-
tails of that call which was to change my life, give it its final
shape.

The date was November 22, 1948. When the phone rang
I glanced toward the door of my small office, which looked
out on my secretary's even smaller one. As New York Supervising Agent I rated a secretary, or rather a clerk, who could
take shorthand and typewrite. The clerk's desk was empty. I
gave the two special agents who had been conferring with me
a small look of apology and a helpless shrug. We had little
enough time to work out the details of the really dangerous

[32]

assignment ahead of us that afternoon without annoying interruptions. I glanced at the clock. It was 9:50 A.M. I picked up the phone and said hello as noncommittally as possible.

"Mr. Baughman?" an operator's voice asked and I admitted my identity. "Mr. Maloney calling from Washington." And James Maloney, then Chief of the Secret Service, was on the phone. He omitted any complimentary salutation. "This is Jim speaking," he said. "Now listen. There's a plane to Washington from La Guardia in fifty minutes. Get on it. Don't stop for anything. Just run downstairs right now and get into a cab and get down here."

He hung up, cutting off my shocked protests before I could get them out. I *couldn't* go. I just couldn't. What about the plan for that afternoon? I looked at my two agents helplessly. The counterfeiting case we'd been conferring on had taken several months to build up and it looked as if we might have one of the largest and most dangerous false-money rings of the year well within the net. I'd know for sure at four that afternoon, for two of my men had an appointment to meet a certain John Arneau, often known as the Frenchman, the ringleader of the gang, in a downtown New York hotel room at that time. They had convinced him, after much hard work, that they were bona fide criminals and that they were going to buy $150,000 worth of really beautifully made counterfeit ten- and twenty-dollar bills for a stipulated price of $15,000 in real money. Three other agents and I were to wait, unbeknownst to Arneau, in a room next to his and make the arrest after the counterfeit money had actually been turned over.

I stood up. "I have to go to Washington," I said to the agents.

[33]

One of them groaned. "Now?" he asked. "Today?"

"Yes," I said. And then I explained. "That was the Chief."

"Oh," they both said and nodded.

"You know what to do," I said. "Just be careful. Just don't give the Frenchman a second after he realizes he's been had. He's going to be awful mad."

I worried all the way out to the airport in the cab. I knew my men were quite capable of carrying the whole affair off without me. The thing that bothered me was my knowledge of just how dangerous Arneau was. He'd shot himself out of a trap once before; and once he'd broken jail, killing a guard. I should be in at the climactic moment.

I recall that Disraeli once said: "I've never really *accomplished* anything. The few things that may have got done under my supervision I've simply *worried* into being." He could have been speaking about me. Not that I show the worry. I'm at least as poker-faced as Dizzy was, but my mind has a habit of racing along a hundred paths, spying out possible eventualities. In the plane I kept going over and over the Arneau case in my mind, worrying it like a dog worries a bone, right up till the moment I stood in front of the Chief's desk, and then his words substituted a whole different set of worries, driving Arneau and everything else out of my mind completely. "The boss wants to see you," he said.

The "boss" was the Secretary of the Treasury. At that time it was John W. Snyder, and though I'd seen him from a distance I had never gotten within hailing distance of him.

"What does he want?" I asked.

"He'll tell you," he said. "Better get right up there."

What was that note I detected in the Chief's voice? Pity?

[34]

An unwillingness to tell me some bad news? What had I done? On the way to the Secretary's office my mind raced over a score of possible gaffes I could have made. If the New York office was in trouble, as the Supervising Agent I certainly would be the goat. We were the biggest Secret Service field office in the country. Counterfeiting had been growing enormously in the past year; and check-forging looked as though it was going to be double, triple, quadruple what it had been. Was I going to be blamed for that? That would be very unfair. It wasn't my job to prevent crime! I was supposed to catch counterfeiters, not reform them!

I didn't have to wait a second in the Secretary's outer office; I was ushered immediately into his presence. He was a kind, fatherly-looking man, relaxed. He came directly to the point, so directly indeed that my mind, filled with its customary scrutiny of possible disasters, did not register his words. "Mr. Maloney is going to a different job, Mr. Baughman," he said, "and I wish to offer you his position as next Chief of the Secret Service. Will you accept?"

The question actually sounded like an accusation, so prepared was I for something quite different. I was dazed at the import of his words. He looked at me and smiled at my wordlessness. "I think I know how you feel," he said. "I felt the same way when Mr. Truman offered me this job. And so did Mr. Truman when he got his job."

I smiled weakly in response to this sympathetic approach to my perturbation. The Secretary continued. "Will you accept?" he said.

I found my voice. "Oh, yes. Yes, sir. I will. Yes, sir," I said.

"Good," said Secretary Snyder. "Done and done. Report

November 29—as Chief." And he put out his hand and shook mine.

I was on the plane by 3 P.M. on my way back to New York. As soon as we took off from the National Airport and I looked down upon the great sprawling and beautiful pattern of Washington, the whole hasty incident I had been through took on a more and more dreamlike quality. Had it really happened at all? Does a man's fate change so drastically in such a quick, unheralded, unpredictable manner? I couldn't really grasp the matter at all.

And then apprehension began to set in; before we were over Baltimore I had come to feel that my affirmative answer to Secretary Snyder's question had been thoughtless, idiotic, absolutely wrong. I had made a terrible mistake!

Who was I to undertake such an enterprise? I was a good agent, certainly. Even a good administrator. But this job was far too big for me. Wasn't it? And was it my cup of tea? They hadn't even given me time to think about such things. They'd forced me to make a snap decision. I began to get angry inside. The thing I'd really liked about the Secret Service, what had kept me in it for twenty years, had been the excitement and the rewards of chasing the counterfeiter, the direct contact with the criminal, matching myself, my brains and sometimes my brawn, against theirs. Certainly I'd loved being a Secret Service agent. But—heading up the whole thing!

I sat still and listened to my thoughts. And then I realized I wasn't facing up to the truth, the real reason why I felt so overwhelmed by the sudden change in my life. It wasn't the shock of my sudden elevation professionally, because I'd now be one of the top law enforcement officers in the country. Nor was it because, as I was trying to tell myself, I wouldn't be chasing counterfeiters any more; actually, I'd be chasing them more than ever; and I'd have the whole nation to chase 'em in, not just the New York area.

No, the real reason, when I faced it, for feeling shaky and uncertain was plain and simple. What bothered me basically was the awful responsibility involved in my new duty of protecting the President of the United States and his family. This was, I knew, a life-and-death burden which the Chief of the Secret Service has to carry with him every day and every night of his life. There is no respite. He may never drop the burden, let it rest on somebody else's shoulders. It is his responsibility and his alone.

Only a very few people know a fact that every Secret Service man learns at once. It is that *the life of the President of the United States is in very real and constant danger. This danger has grown in recent years and will grow even more in the future.*

That is no melodramatic statement. Nor is it the slightest bit exaggerated. You know that three of our Presidents have already been assassinated—and that the assassins were insane. But did you know that five others have come within a hair's-breadth of being murdered by mad individuals? Or that innumerable threats have been sent to Presidential incumbents from the days of Washington to the present?

Or that scores and scores of other attempts have been made on the lives of our Presidents? These receive little or no space in the papers, for they usually don't get very far off the ground.

But that is only because of the Secret Service, and its constant, unwearying vigilance.

Who makes these attempts, the successful ones, the near-successful ones and the complete failures? They are all made by mentally disturbed people. You have already seen one of these mentally disturbed people in action, the insane Pavlick and his attempt on the life of President Kennedy.

There are fifty thousand potential Pavlicks in the United States today. We have their insane letters on file, letters which threaten the lives of the President and his family. A whole special division of the Secret Service is kept constantly at work tracking these letters down, uncovering their authors, who are usually anonymous, and keeping them under surveillance.

Yes, the mad are a dagger, a Damoclean sword that hangs continually over the First Family's heads. The mad not only write, they often come in person. Sometimes they demand to see the President, smirking and grinning their madness at the White House gates. We can be certain of handling them when they announce themselves and their insanity but sometimes they do not. Sometimes they wait till night and sneak over the White House fence, snake along the grass. Often they are armed, carry knives or guns.

As individuals they are sometimes capable of the most cunning kind of planning. Sometimes they are intellectuals. Sometimes their mental condition is cloaked in the disguise of a political philosophy. But whatever mask he uses, the assassin, underneath, is insane. In the Secret Service we have found that to be unfailingly true.

I will have more to tell you about these potential killers and how we guard against them. For the moment, however, it is enough to say that my disturbing indecisiveness on the plane was due to the dreadful danger they constitute.

It was with such thoughts that I at length arrived at La Guardia. I had completely forgotten to call my office about the counterfeiter Arneau—which is a very clear measure of how far up in the clouds I was. Every government agent knows you just don't forget such matters.

I went home then, my mind a whirling mass of confusion and contradictory decisions. My wife opened the door and when she saw me I noticed the color drain from her face. "What's happened?" she said. "You look awful."

I waited for a moment and then, in a sepulchral tone, I said: "I'm the next Chief of the Secret Service."

She looked at me a long time, at first in disbelief, then with a milder doubt and then with dawning comprehension. Finally she smiled. "Come in," she said, knowing, as always, exactly what had happened to me. She took me by the arm and pulled me in the door. "It could be worse," she said. "They might have made you Secretary of the Treasury."

I laughed a little at that, a sign that my own sanity would undoubtedly return sooner or later. However, it was at least two hours before she had convinced me that it was okay to be scared. She even, in the end, convinced me that maybe we had something to celebrate about and went out and got us some champagne to do just that. So we celebrated and as the hours went by I could feel my confidence seeping back into me, but slowly.

Oh, I finally did call the office, thank heavens. The agents were there with Arneau and had been there since 5 P.M. and it was nine before I called. They'd gotten him easily, with three of his confederates. There was no question the ring was smashed. "It went off like clockwork, just as you planned it," the agent told me.

"Thanks," I said, pleasantly aware of the subtle flattery in the "just as you planned it." "Good work. Hold them overnight. I'll see you in the morning."

But the whole case seemed awfully anticlimactic to me.

Inaugural Dangers

I AM TALKING TO PRESIDENT TRUMAN, STANDING beside the long White House swimming pool. It is my second day on my new job and I have just been introduced to Mr. Truman by Jim Rowley, who heads up the branch of the Secret Service known as the White House Detail, a group of some forty hand-picked agents who are always with the President and who are chiefly responsible for his safety. The President is grinning at me, dripping wet from a plunge in the pool, looking at me in that kind, reassuring way he has.

"I'm pleased to meet you, U.E.," he said, using the initials my friends call me by, though I don't know how he found out they constituted my nickname. "I've heard a lot of good things about you."

"Thank you, Mr. President," I said, trying to appear at ease in his presence. I wasn't yet used to such intimacy with the famous.

"You have one of the hardest jobs in Washington," he said, now with great earnestness. "And I want you to know I realize that fact. Anything I can do to ease it for you . . ." he left the sentence unfinished.

There was a slight pause and then, dropping his serious manner, as I was to see him do so often in the future when any undue solemnity began to intrude itself: "Just remember," he grinned, "it won't be half as tough on you as the job they handed me a few years ago."

Basically, of course, he was right and his kind words helped me a great deal, but for a while, as I grappled with the problems of protecting the President and accustoming myself to the prosecution of crime on a national basis rather than on the local or regional scale I was used to, my new job seemed infinitely ramified, as difficult as any job could get, and I found it hard to imagine that even Harry Truman's could have been more troublesome or perplexing to him at the start.

My new office was in the Treasury Building right next door to my new charge in the White House. It was a large, grand-looking room with a huge desk that contained a bewildering array of telephones. Next to it was my own dressing room. I was bowled over by all the elegance. But my chief new acquisition was a real live secretary, not a Secret Service clerk in disguise. Well, secretary is not quite the word for her. Miss Edith E. Duncan has been my good right arm and sometimes my left one too, a wonderful person, to whom I owe far too much even to try to thank. She was with me during my entire term as Chief.

Now that I have come to grips with the main part of my story I want to explain something. It is that I am tempted to try to tell about everybody and everything at once. I want to tell of all the branches of the Secret Service and what they do; of the fabulous White House Detail, the Protective Research Detail, the White House Police, the Treasury Guard Force, the Counterfeiting Section, the Check-Forging Bureau and all the other branches.

I know I must resist that temptation. It would get boring if I told everything at once. So I am going to try to let the information come gradually, as my own story unfolds, much as I myself learned about and began to master the varied techniques and skills of the Secret Service.

This is by far the more natural, and therefore the more interesting way to proceed. It is more natural for, at this juncture, I was a real beginner as far as Presidential protection goes. Knowledgeable as I was about counterfeiting and related crimes, my experience with securing the safety of a President could be summed up in a few incidents, mostly funny ones.

There was the time, for example that Herbert Hoover had come to Philadelphia in 1928. Assigned to help protect him at the Bellevue Stratford Hotel (the local branch of the Secret Service is often called upon to help out whenever a President visits its district), I determined to look my very best in front of the great man. To this end I dressed myself to the nines in my gaudiest Sunday best; a light brown suit and a green shirt with a matching green tie. The agents from Washington who traveled with the President took one look at their eager young helper and put me behind the potted palms in the rear of the mezzanine. I never did get to see Hoover outside of the newsreels.

The fact is that the men who protect the President must dress conservatively, in dark, well-tailored clothes; for inconspicuousness, it should be self-evident, is a prime necessity. Such sobriety in taste, however, was a hard virtue for me to acquire. A picture taken of me as late as 1936 showed me in front of FDR's Inaugural stand peering out into the crowd for any would-be assassins, dressed in a flamboyant new camel's hair coat. On my head was a smart new snap-brim fedora, a pearl-gray beacon among the forest of seemly black Homburgs surrounding me. I always look a little lonely to myself, and a little sad, in that snapshot.

Actually I only began to envisage the very complicated problems inherent in protecting the great and those near and dear to them when I became Supervising Agent in New York. Margaret Truman moved there in 1947 to take up her singing career professionally and I was asked to join with the White House Detail in inaugurating a permanent over-all protective plan to insure her safety, for, as I have already noted, not only the President himself but his entire family, up to and including his in-laws, was our responsibility. In President Truman's case some odd and even quite amusing situations developed from this fact, which involved not only Margaret but Mrs. Truman's three brothers and the President's older sister, Mary, an unmarried lady, who loved fast cars. I will come to their stories later.

Protecting Margaret in her New York hotel, however—and

even going down to Puerto Rico, as I did on one occasion on a special assignment to sniff out any possible danger from the Nationalist Party—this was only the beginning of the beginning of what I had to learn about Presidential protection.

In practice such protection is not only a complex matter—it's almost infinitely ramified, it is eternal vigilance squared. The fact is that we give our Presidents the most complete, detailed and expert protection of any country in the world. We leave out nothing that science or art or know-how can supply to the task.

Let us start then with my first real task as Chief—preparing for President Truman's security during his Inaugural week. It is a major job and, as you observed during the Kennedy festivities, makes the Chief of the Secret Service still worry even after he's become very experienced in such matters.

The fact is that inauguration time can be a period of particular danger. This is first of all because of the huge crowds the President and his family must move among. Compounding the danger is the fact that the Chief Executive will be going to specific places and moving along specified routes at times that can be ascertained by anybody.

As people are beginning to learn from television, the actual Inauguration is only one event in a series of festivities that last for almost a week. The Truman Inauguration celebrations were all the more intense and crowded because of the dramatic defeat Mr. Truman had administered to his Republican opponent, Thomas Dewey, all predictions to the contrary.

Here is a schedule of the week's events, or at least the major ones that the President and/or Bess and Margaret were to attend.

[45]

Jan. 18—The Truman-Barkley Club dinner at the Mayflower Hotel.

Jan. 19—Breakfast for the President at the Metropolitan
Club. Huge luncheon at the Mayflower. After-
noon reception at the Shoreham Hotel. Huge
Electoral College dinner at the Mayflower. Huge
Gala Concert at the National Guard Armory.

Jan. 20—Breakfast at the Shoreham Hotel. Inauguration
ceremony in front of the Capitol; the Inaugural
Parade; the Inaugural Reception at the National
Gallery; the tremendous Inaugural Ball at the
National Guard Armory.

Jan. 21—A mammoth reception at the Wardman Park
Hotel.

The security measures planned for these festivities filled a
one-thousand-page book. This book was made available to all
members of the Secret Service involved and to ranking members of the armed services and police departments co-operat-
ing with us. It would be impossible to give all the details of
these plans and measures but some of the highlights are
interesting.

Here are a few of the security measures called for:

Every manhole and sewer along the route of the Inaugural
Parade had to be sealed; the slowness of the vehicles in the
parade (three miles an hour) and the fact the route is so well
known would have made it relatively easy for an assassin to
place dynamite in a sewer and detonate it as the President's
car passed over it.

[46]

Every single building and all of its occupants along the parade route had to be checked. We had to have a dossier on each occupant sufficient to guarantee that he was "safe." Only then could we grant him the privilege of viewing the parade from his window or his rooftop.

This was really a mighty job in itself if you consider the matter. The route of the Inaugural Parade started at the Pennsylvania Avenue entrance of the White House, and wound its slow way to Capitol Hill. There were literally hundreds of buildings along the route and thousands of tenants.

Were our precautions excessive? No. They were absolutely necessary. The President and his First Lady would ride these streets in an open car at a speed of three miles an hour. As the hundreds of thousands of people roared and waved and applauded, both of them would have been sitting ducks for a determined lunatic in a window even if he were a relatively poor shot. So thorough was the check we made that on Inauguration Day, as I rode in the Chief's limousine immediately ahead of the car carrying Harry and Bess Truman, I could look up to the people waving from the windows and the housetops and almost manage a confident smile. I felt as if I knew each of those enthusiastic arm-wavers personally, and in the sense of having a dossier on each one I did.

When most people think of a hotel banquet, even a large one, they think of a ballroom with a hundred or perhaps two hundred, at most five hundred guests. An Inaugural week dinner attended by the President runs into the thousands. And other events are comparably outsized.

To give the range: the Gala Concert at the Armory (an exclusively white-tie affair) had 5,300 invited guests! And the Truman-Barkley Club dinner at the Mayflower Hotel, a relatively minor function, had 2,100 black-tie invitees!

I mention these sizes to give some idea of the scope of the security measures required, for of course, the larger the crowd surrounding the President, the greater opportunity a would-be assassin has of slipping in and getting close to him. And the greater opportunity, too, such an assassin has, amid the confusion created by such crowds, of plotting other types of dangerous mischief—severing a cable on an elevator car the President will ride, weakening a chandelier over the Presidential table, starting a fire, etc.

We must keep every possibility in mind and hence our security precautions become extremely elaborate. To show the measures we take, let us use the Truman-Barkley Club dinner as an example. If you then multiply the steps we took to make that event "secure" by the number of events the President attends during Inaugural week, you will get a rough picture of some of our activities during that crowded social season.

Secret Service plans for the Truman-Barkley Club dinner were laid weeks ahead, as they were for all these festivities. The route the President would travel from the White House to the Mayflower was mapped out; the door of the hotel he'd debark at was decided upon; the car he would ride in was chosen; the type of guard necessary for the streets feeding into his route and the route itself were selected; the corridors he must walk through in the Mayflower were picked out; the number of agents who would accompany him at each point of his journey decided upon. All that could possibly be foreseen and planned for far in advance was done.

[48]

A few days before the dinner a security check was made on all hotel personnel who would come into contact with the President before, during and after the dinner.

Bellboys were investigated. All the waiters at the dinner had to be "cleared." The waiters who were to serve the President himself had to be men who not only had received a more-than-thorough security check but had waited on the President before.

All the cooks, too, had to be completely cleared. If a security clearance could not be obtained on an individual cook before the banquet the services of that cook were dispensed with for the occasion.

I should say here that a Secret Service security clearance is not merely political. It is chiefly psychological. We are mainly concerned with the mental balance of the individual, for even an extreme radical, in our experience, will not assassinate a man he hates politically unless he has a major disorder in his thinking, a mental disturbance. Our men have become very, very expert in picking out mental disturbances in an individual, and some of them can sense it nearly as well as a psychiatrist can. These are the men who have had experience with the lunatic fringe we encounter constantly at the White House gates and through the mails.

The food to be cooked for the banquet was carefully examined the day before the dinner. Samples of each item to be eaten were sent to a laboratory for an analysis. They all passed their tests. Thereafter a permanent guard was kept on the food till it had been placed before Mr. Truman and Mr. Barkley. I was prepared on this occasion to guarantee every mouthful our Chief Executive ate, since I myself oversaw the lab analysis of the food and stationed the guard after it had been made.

On the morning of the banquet a special team of Secret Service agents swarmed over the hotel. The elevators the President and the Veep (as they used to call Vice President Barkley) were to ride were thoroughly checked and inspected. A guard was then put at the entrance leading to the mechanism of these elevators and another at the master switches which controlled them, and these guards stayed on duty till the President left the hotel.

Another Secret Service team carefully inspected the entire banquet area for time bombs, radioactive materials and fire hazards. The moorings of a heavy chandelier were inspected to see that it would not, by accident or design, fall on our charges.

The President was to arrive at 6:40. Promptly at 5:30 I had Secret Service agents clear the entire area in which the banquet would take place.

Stray souls wandering about, waiters preparing the tables, everybody was ushered out of this section. Then a single gateway was established through which the outside world must pass to get into the banquet. Every other possible entryway was sealed off. When this had been achieved, the help preparing the banquet were, one by one, reidentified and allowed to return to their duties.

We then followed this up by rechecking the banquet area for bombs and even possible assassins. This included a second look in all closets and even under the tables. As this was going on agents and detectives took up their stations at every single possible entrance to the banquet section of the hotel.

There were eighty men in all at these stations. I had arranged them in a concentric pattern, the thinnest line being on the outer circle and the thickest closest to the banquet hall. This was the traditional pattern by which agents surround the President wherever he may be. The theory is that any attack will have to penetrate layer after concentric layer of defenders, the heaviest layer of defense, of course, being closest to the President.

I was on hand to oversee these preparations personally. I had no heart for delegating responsibilities in those first weeks of my new job. This helped me, for I learned a great deal by being on the spot. At six o'clock I went over to the White House to pick up the President. Our route to the hotel, as had been planned weeks before, was now cleared of all cars and the traffic on the side streets deflected till we had passed. At 6:22 the President got into his limousine at Blair House and with cars full of Secret Service agents fore and aft, all armed of course, he sped to the banquet.

One more interesting point. How could we be sure that a ringer still could not get into the banquet by counterfeiting a pass to the affair? No guarantee is absolutely perfect. However, we had two safeguards against such an attempt. One was to design the admission ticket ourselves and to oversee its printing. We are, after all, experts in counterfeiting matters. Also, we assigned three agents with long experience in detecting and studying counterfeits to be the ticket-takers. Anybody trying to pass phony versions of our tickets had very little chance of fooling this elite body of hawk-eyed ticket-takers.

My precautions also called for agents in full dress to be spotted throughout the hall, passing as guests. There was one at every table and though he might be smiling and talking, his eyes ceaselessly examined the people about him for any strange or suspicious moves toward the guests of honor.

I too sat among the guests. The following conversation is one I had with a fellow guest and it shows, I trust, how nicely we agents blended with our surroundings.

He was a red-faced, slightly pompous, minor official and he said to me. "You may not realize it but there are several Secret Service agents here in tuxedos."

"There are?" I said.

"Certainly," he said in his Colonel Blimp manner, "there always are. I know because I know their faces."

"Where are they?" I asked.

He nodded in the direction of a guest at our table. "He's one," he said, "the first on the left across the table, the fellow with the crew cut and the pink rosette in his lapel."

I looked at the man he was pointing to in wonder. "Really?" I said.

"Oh, yes," he said. "They're a fine-looking bunch of men. Some of them are educated. You'd never know them from one of us."

"Is that true?" I exclaimed in astonishment.

Gratified by my reactions, he pointed out a few of the others. I did not know any of the gentlemen he indicated and I have never seen any of them again. But in my heart I forgave him because of his high regard for our fine-looking cadre and for the extent to which some of us had been educated.

Well, these are some of the highlights of the measures we used to protect the President at this single banquet—up to and including the measure of keeping calm when certain members of the party become, however unintentionally, a little insulting. From these notes you will perhaps get some idea of the variety of pressures on the Secret Service during Inauguration week. Consider that we had to put these or similar protective plans into effect for every single festivity attended by the President—and you will realize how busy we were.

Learning this rich and varied lore of Presidential protection at the same time as I was practicing it was a tremendous nervous strain at the beginning. I did not, during this whole Inaugural period, relax for a moment. But then, at long last, the end was near. The final festive occasion was the huge reception at the Wardman Park Hotel. I remember well my feelings as, after I had taken the President to his door with the First Lady, he turned to me and said, again using my initials: "You've done a nice job, U.E. I really appreciate it." I thanked him and he smiled and they turned and went in.

I breathed a deep sigh of relief. I had weathered the first test and suddenly I didn't feel tense or even tired any more. I felt as if I could stay up all night, take on a whole inauguration again, singlehanded. It's amazing how invigorating a little praise from the President of the United States can be!

chapter 5

The Dangerous Cranks

ONE MORNING I ARRIVED AT MY OFFICE TO FIND
an urgent message from President Truman. I checked at once
and found that he was very disturbed about a letter that had
been sent to Margaret. It was a passionate communication and
proposed that the sender and Mr. Truman's daughter get married posthaste. It was unsigned and no return address was
given. The President wanted me to see if I could find out who
this individual was and whether or not he was dangerous.

I myself brought this letter to what we call our Protective
Research section. Within an hour I was back on the phone to
the White House. We'd been able to find out who had sent

this missive of connubial hope, I was able to inform the President, and I could assure him that the poor fellow was harmless.

Mr. Truman, just as quickly, sent back a message to me congratulating the Secret Service on its efficiency and stating that ours was the promptest service he had ever obtained from a government agency.

Earlier I mentioned that the central danger to the President and his family came from some fifty thousand mentally disturbed people in this country. The dimensions of the danger these people pose had made me wish for a short time that I had not accepted my appointment as Chief from Secretary Snyder. I should like to tell now something about these people, who they are, and what they are suffering from that makes us feel they are such a threat. Only when one knows the full shocking story about them will the never-ending caution of the Secret Service, the seemingly excessively protective measures we take, be properly understood.

The control of the mentally disturbed is the work, as I just mentioned, of our Protective Research section. It is headed by Robert Bouck, a great Secret Service agent. Protective Research is one of the most unique and highly efficient detective centers in the world. It is, in effect, the central bastion in our defense-in-depth of the President and his family against the assassin, a clearinghouse for every individual in the United States who could be considered a potential danger to the First Family.

The names of these people come to our attention in a wide variety of ways. A bartender may overhear a customer threatening to kill the President; he feels that there might be something to this threat and he reports him to us. Or governmental law enforcement agencies may get wind of a potential assassin or of a political group we should watch and the information is turned over to us. Worried neighbors, friends or relatives may report to us threats they have heard. Sometimes the neighbor or friend is the person we find most worthy of our concern. We assess and assay each report and, if we feel it warranted, we investigate. In every case a full record of the results goes into our files.

Basically, however, the fifty thousand odd records in our files are of people who have written threatening or obscene letters to the President or his family, or who have appeared at the White House and attempted to see the President or to attack him.

Let me give you a look into one of the scores of file drawers on such people. I will select a folder from one of these drawers at random to show the explosive, wild, distorted kinds of minds we are dealing with here.

It contains ten letters from a man in California. Here is the address he sent one of them to:

TO: HARRY THE KIKE
President of the Jewnited STATES
WASH. (your dirty linen in public)
D.C. (Dirty Communist)

I can't print the contents of the letter in this envelope; it is too obscene. Each of the ten letters is equally vile. They are all unsigned of course and there is no return address. But we know this character, everything about him.

Let's look at the next folder. It's from a woman from Massachusetts. There are three letters all properly addressed. Here is a sample of the contents of one:

DEAR PRESIDENT: Me no Lie, tell 'em heap big Truth, UG! ug! Uh. Huh. You know whether me lie or not and chief witnesses Christ wasn't born in a King's Palace But A Manger You Know. The Last Place You Would Expect Minnie Ha Ha and Hiawatha In St. Louis State Hospital. Sink my Life Line In Phony Valentine Program Jan-May Compass. Lived across the Street from Valentine.

This absolutely senseless drivel goes on for pages. It's unsigned of course but we have a complete dossier on the writer.

Here's another folder next to it. This one is addressed to "Harry Trumman, the Wite Huse." Its message:

DEAR SIR: only these few lines to let yo no that I am stell in Dallas. I nede 5000 pleez at once or I will kill.

Rifling at random now through the drawer we get the full flavor. It is amazing how clearly this kind of lunacy is connected with racial hatred of the most virulent kind.

Address: To that full blooded Jew Sherman Adams, White House, Washington, D.C.
Message: What are you baldheaded jews doing down there.

Address: To the Nigger Loving President of the Jewnited States
Message: You will be judged in heaven if you help those black apes. And I may put you there.

Some of the letters sound like the resounding laughter in a madhouse, the ravings in the back wards where the incurable and violent are kept. Here is one to our President from a New Orleans Ophelia:

I! Love! The! Dear! Silver!
That! Shines! In! Your! Hair!
Oh such great stuff—He! Ha!
Hay! Ho! God Love Ike and Mike.

Some, with their confused and cloudy messages, are terribly pathetic. Here's one from an older woman in Florida.

I am rite you to find out what I can do with Lawyer Bruten for forge deads on my land and property to Charlie Mayfield and lillie Mayfield his wife. And not let me no nothing about. Charlie Mayfield and his wife both has been in sane silem in New York years ago and now he call me crazy and forge papers and deads on my land and titles on my car to. [This goes on for pages and asks the Secret Service if it won't help in having several people killed for her or else she will kill the President.]

And here's a letter to the President that is forty feet long, full of incomprehensible gibberish and threats. Here is another only three words long. It is on a tiny piece of paper. All three words are four-letter obscenities.

Perhaps, as you look at these letters, you wonder if such people can actually be dangerous. They sometimes sound merely pathetic—or disgusting. The fact is, and experience has proven it time after time, they can and will kill and usually they give warning of that fact. These letters are the warnings. Our chief job is to pick up these warnings before any harm is done.

The potential President-killer among the population, for the most part, suffers from a particular disease. It used to be called "dementia praecox" but the later terminology for it is "schizophrenia with paranoid delusions." The danger from such people increases as their illness deepens. And here's the tragic part; this kind of mental affliction usually gets worse, slowly and insidiously, sometimes taking years.

In the beginning the letters these people send to the President will often sound innocuous enough—and they frequently sign them at this early juncture. There will be some mild complaint about a Presidential policy or the like. Any good American, with firm convictions about his government, might have written it. But, when the person is ill, other letters will follow and, finally, one will contain an obscenity or a threat to the President's life. We have records of certain people whose slow deterioration has lasted for two decades and can be seen by their correspondence, each melancholy step of it. In 99 per cent of all cases where there has been a threat or an obscenity the letter is from a person with a serious mental disturbance.

Of course all paranoid schizophrenics are not potential President-killers. The ones who are, are those whose delusions have become "fixed" on the office of the Presidency. We say they have a "Presidential complex." It isn't the President as a person they wish to assassinate. They wish to kill the "office," the visible sign of the authority they believe is persecuting them.

Joseph Zangara, who attempted to kill President Roosevelt in Florida, is a clear example of this. He had first intended to assassinate President Hoover in 1932. But FDR was elected and Zangara switched his attentions to the President-elect. His bullet did not get the new President but it did kill Anton Cermak, Mayor of Chicago, who was riding in the seat next to Roosevelt.

Anybody who doubts that the people who threaten the life of the President are as insidiously dangerous as I say should

[59]

look at the vast store of information the Secret Service has accumulated on successful assassins of public figures throughout the world in the past hundred years. It would convince them at once.

I am only going to take one historic example, however, for the whole problem shows up with eminent clarity in this case. It is that of Charles Guiteau, an obscure seeker of a minor office in the government. His "Presidential complex" can be seen perfectly in a series of communiqués written before and after his murder of President Garfield in 1881. (Remember, as you read Guiteau's words, the letters found on Pavlick after he attempted to kill President-Elect Kennedy not very long ago.)

1. From a letter found on the street immediately after the fatal attack on Garfield. It was addressed to General Sherman:

I have just shot the President. . . . His death was a political necessity. I am a lawyer, theologian and politician. I am a stalwart of the Stalwarts. . . . I am going to the jail. Please order out the troops and take possession of the jail at once. Yours respectfully, Charles Guiteau.

2. From a letter taken from Guiteau after the attack:

To the White House. The President's death was a sad necessity; but it will unite the Republican Party and save the Republic. Life is a flimsy dream, and it matters little when one goes. A human life is of small value. . . . He was liable to go at any time anyway. I had no ill-will toward the President. His death was a political necessity.

3. Guiteau went downhill mentally very fast after his insane act. Here is a note from his autobiography, which was published in the newspapers after his imprisonment. It gives a

disconcertingly sharp view of the topography of madness and makes one realize how long an incubation period such acts have:

> For twenty years I have had an idea that I should be President. I had the idea when I lived in the Oneida Community [a settlement by a Utopian sect in upstate New York] and it has never left me. When I left Boston for New York in June, 1880, I remember distinctly I felt that I was on my way to the White House. . . . My idea is that I shall be nominated and elected as Lincoln and Garfield were—that is, by an act of God. If I were President, I should seek to give the Nation a first-class Administration in every respect. My object would be to unify the entire American people, and make them happy, prosperous and God-fearing.

Today, any letter which Guiteau would have written to the President before he acted would undoubtedly have come into our hands and we would have been able to prevent the whole horrible chain of events.

And this brings us to just how our Protection Research section operates. Let us start at the beginning, for our methods, from the standpoint of catching the criminal, are unusual ones.

In the first place, all the President's mail is screened by specially trained personnel in the White House Mail Room. These individuals send all threatening or obscene letters to Protective Research—about fifteen hundred a month! One of our main chores then is to classify and process these epistles. We keep a filing system of two million cards on which we note every detail of each letter we receive.

Our system is based on the knowledge that a person who writes a threatening or abusive letter to the President is generally a repeater. He's written one before or he will again.

If he's a one-shot man he usually isn't dangerous. But in almost every case we can find out who he is even if he sends only one letter. When he sends two or more our batting average is 98 per cent. Here is how we maintain that average.

First step: Every piece of mail we get is examined with awesome thoroughness by a highly trained agent. He fills out a twenty-four-question form on each letter, listing whether it was written in ink, pencil, by typewriter or with a crayon. Misspelled words are noted, any mention of a geographical area, unique words or phrases, peculiarities in crossing t's or dotting i's, or making capitals, or hyphenating words—all are carefully listed.

Next the agent "psychoanalyzes" the letter, so to speak, noting evidence of active hallucinations or obsessions or of systematic delusions of persecution. The latter symptom is particularly dangerous. Such people feel that they are going to be attacked or killed by imaginary enemies and may try to kill somebody before these "enemies" can get to them. It is also noted in this analysis just what obscenities and threats, and the degree and extent of them, have been used. Such observations are helpful in diagnosing the illness and also in identifying the particular individual.

Unusual types of ink are also noted. They can often be traced to their manufacturer and thus to the location of the retailers who purchased them. And all envelopes are saved— for at least the words "Washington, D.C." must be on them when they are addressed to the President and thus we can compare the handwriting of these recurring words on other envelopes. This is particularly helpful when the contents of the letter are brief.

[62]

When all this is done the agent now tries to find out if the writer is a repeater. The chances, as I have said, are very great that he is. Careful cross files of every identifying peculiarity noted above are now consulted and the attempt is made to match the letter with one we already have on file. The fact that the letter is not signed isn't important; its peculiarities will identify the sender in almost all cases.

Let's take a typical example. A letter has come in addressed to "Hairy Truman—The Ape President—Washington, D.C." It is handwritten and has a sentence in it that reads: "I will pierce you with the Prophet's sword of Righteousness, you godamned hypocrite." And it has a small symbol of a hand drawn in red ink that stands for the signature.

In this case the agent first goes to the file on symbols and selects letter specimens of all those people who have sent letters with red-inked hands drawn on them. Then he selects specimens of all those who have used the phrases "ape" or "hairy ape" in letters to the President. Next he selects specimens of people whose letters have the foregoing characteristics and who also combine Biblical phraseology such as "Prophet's sword of Righteousness" with profanity. By now our man has narrowed the field down considerably, perhaps has an almost absolute fix on the suspect.

At this point the handwriting on the letter we have just received is compared with that of the suspects in our file who fit the bill in other particulars. To an expert this type of comparison can be the clincher, and it almost always turns out to be the handwriting on the wall for the sender of the letter. If he's a repeater his whereabouts have probably already been discovered and I now send out word to the Secret Service office nearest to the offender's home to have him checked out. Frequently, if he has not been sent to a mental institution, he must now be.

But, you may ask, if the person hasn't written before and if his letter is anonymous, how do we locate him in the first place? To do that we use every modern sleuthing trick in the book. Here's a case that's fairly typical of our approach. I call it "The Case of the Cracked O."

Not too long ago we received a letter containing the line: "I am going to kill you Mr. President." It had been mailed in Arkansas from a town we'll call Pennsville. We put it through our "system" and found that this was a "first" for the writer.

Now we ascertained, from an examination of the type, that the typewriter on which it had been written was a portable. A further scrutiny of the letters with a microscope showed that the lower case "o" had a small crack in it. The lead was a slim one, but slimmer ones often had led to pay dirt.

At this juncture we photographed the "o" and made blowups of the pictures. These were sent posthaste to the Secret Service office nearest to Pennsville, Arkansas. This was our Little Rock office. I sent instructions to my men there to contact the sheriff and the post office personnel in Pennsville and to give them copies of our blowups. Also, I asked them to contact newspapers, especially the "letters-to-the-editor" departments (for paranoids often send their letters to such places), and to give the editors our pictures of the "o."

Action was slow. Half a year passed before our break finally came. The postmaster at Pennsville had noticed a typed letter addressed to a letters-to-the-editor department of a near-by newspaper. Our agents were called in and the newspaper editor opened the letter in their presence and then handed it over to them for their perusal. Sure enough, a magnifying glass showed the cracked "o." It was identical with the one in the letter to the President. But, most important, there was a return address on the envelope.

The writer of the letter turned out to be a housewife with three children. She was cracking up mentally, however, as a thorough psychiatric examination showed, and might have been dangerous, not only to the President but to her own children. She was institutionalized and we have kept tabs on her since. I am glad to report that she seems to have responded to therapy.

Have you ever, in a burst of gratitude or warmth, wanted to send a gift to the President? If you actually send one your spirit will be greatly appreciated but your gift horse will be looked in the mouth by experts.

All packages that come to the White House are fluoroscoped and if their contents are not at once evident or are the slightest bit suspicious (say you've sent a wrist watch and it ticks) they are X-rayed. If the contents still can't be seen clearly and the Secret Service agents aren't perfectly confident about the gift, it will be carefully toted to the yard outside and placed in a specially constructed bomb-carrier. This is a huge Easter-egg-shaped container made of one-inch-thick cable taken from the elevator shaft of the Washington Monument and carefully braided into an almost indestructable web. This container, which can withstand the blast made by fifty sticks of dynamite, is mounted on a truck and the hot cargo is transported to a remote spot in the country and there torn to pieces with special grappling hooks that can be operated from a distance.

Do we ever get bombs like this? Yes. That's all I can say about it, for security reasons. Except perhaps this:

One humorous character sent Margaret Truman a piece of candy which was set inside one of those party favors, the cylindrical kind with two pieces of paper sticking from either end which, when you pull, make a bang like a cap pistol going off. Only, so much powder was in this "favor" it could have injured the receiver badly, perhaps blinded her. Investigation, however, showed that it was sent by a person above suspicion and with only the best of intentions. Preserve me from this individual if his intentions are ever bad.

Some of the "presents" we receive lead us to people who are quite as dangerous as the ones who send threatening or obscene letters. Many of these send gifts of recordings to the President —recordings they have made personally. These often contain the most objectionable kind of material and of course we screen them thoroughly.

The hardest record we had to screen was a real long-player. It took nine hours of listening to, and it was fascinating in its own morbid way, a mixture of pure mathematics and pure madness. The sender claimed he had a formula for what he called an O (for Optical) bomb, which would cause total destruction of everything everywhere. Much of the record was a recital of the mathematics that he had devised to back up his claim.

For a good part of the record he sounds perfectly rational and you begin to wonder whether this total bomb might not be the McCoy—for you don't know anything about his proofs. In the last hour, however, the insanity shows through. Now he states that all his mathematical secrets have been obtained from the Holy Bible and he states that the Bible, if it were run through a special computer which he alone knows how to make would yield the secret of everything.

Incidentally, he gave his IQ as 450, somewhat higher than Einstein's—or anybody else's—and he told us toward the melancholy close that the work he had been doing had now exhausted even him and that he had been living on coffee and Dexedrine tablets in order to push it through to its conclusion.

Presents sent to the President must be handled with the greatest tact and diplomacy and yet with a hard-headed sense of realism. Most senders, even if insane, are well intentioned, but many wish to exploit the Presidency for personal profit.

For example, one wholesaler sent a pair of shoes to the President. A thank-you letter was sent back on White House stationery. The wholesaler had thousands of copies printed up and sent out to his customers. The clear implication was that the President of the United States used and recommended this product.

This kind of thing of course irritates the Presidential incumbent, whoever he may be. The only time I've personally seen Mr. Eisenhower really mad was when he was shown a copy of a children's book which, on the surface, looked innocent enough. It was written on the subject of the Declaration of Independence in clear, simple prose. The only trouble was that it had an introduction signed by Dwight David Eisenhower. The President had neither written the introduction nor given permission to have his name used. That publisher, I happen to know, was a sorry fellow as a result of his unmitigated gall.

Gifts of food to the President are generally destroyed. The

reason for this is not ingratitude or indifference on the President's part but the simple fact that it is impossible to check on them—or perhaps impracticable would be a better word. For example, if a crate of oranges were sent, a sample from every single orange in the crate would have to be taken and a laboratory test run on each sample before I could have felt justified in clearing it for use by the President or his family. In such a case, of course, the oranges would be ruined by the testing. But even when tests would not ruin the food they would entail too much expense and work. Too, while certain kinds of disturbed people would not perhaps wish to poison the President, they might contaminate their presents in some gross way, say by spitting on the food they sent or putting dirt on it. A chemical analysis would probably not reveal such contamination. Thus when the sender is not known or not thoroughly reliable, the food is usually not examined and not used.

Gifts from friends of the family, of course, are different. When we see the name of a friend on a package of food we simply check with the sender to see if he did indeed send the gift. If he did and if we can establish that the gift hasn't been tampered with, we allow it to go through. If we can't determine that it definitely hasn't been tampered with, we send it to the Pure Food and Drug Administration's laboratory for an analysis.

People who bring or send gifts without return addresses cause a very special headache. For no matter how foolish or unusable they may be, we must keep such gifts during the entire term of the President they are sent to. The reason is that the sender can and often does finally identify himself—sometimes as much as two or three years later. We must be prepared

[68]

to tell him the truth—that his gift, though valued for the spirit behind it, cannot be used by the President. In such a case we wish to be able to return the present in good condition.

During FDR's three terms the accumulation of such objects was great. I didn't see FDR's gifts but Mr. Eisenhower's filled a small warehouse. They ranged from fur-lined foot-warmers to a huge hand-painted wooden eagle and an all-cement, life-size statue of an anonymous woman, probably the giver of the gift.

One of these unsolicited treasures sticks in my mind for some reason. Indeed, when I had a high fever from a bout of the flu it haunted me. It is a large rectangle of wood, I'd say about six feet long and five feet wide. On it is painted in bright, primitive colors a picture of the Deity with a bat in His hands ready to swing at a big sphere. The legend under the fearsome picture reads:

> Our World Is A Ball
> God Is At Bat
> Let Us All Pray Together
> That He May Let Us Pass.

In the febrile nightmare I had during my bout of flu God had decided to take a swat at the oncoming sphere and I woke up screaming.

The handling of mentally disturbed people presents very sensitive problems for the Secret Service. The Protective Research staff must act, unofficially, as psychiatrists; be able to diagnose and to handle psychotic individuals. As I have said, some of them have become almost as good at ferreting out paranoid schizophrenia as the professionals are.

[69]

But of course, legally speaking, none of us has any competence in this area before the law. And we have no rights, nor any wish to have such rights, to commit an individual to a mental institution.

When a person presents himself at the White House gates and acts strangely or offers threats of violence or utters obscenities, we simply call the local police. From them we request a report on the person before he is released. Generally he is held for observation and almost always is committed for a time to a mental institution. We then ask the institution to report regularly on his condition, and also to let us know at once if he escapes or is released. We go through the same procedure for our disturbed letter writers. The local police co-operate with our nearest branch office to see that the individual is investigated and, if necessary, given the proper care. All information on the individual goes right into his file in our central office.

But here's where the "sensitive" part comes in. This is a democracy and we pride ourselves, very properly, on our God-given right to criticize everybody and everything that we find wanting. The Secret Service must be very careful to distinguish between the normal citizen who is merely asserting his right to let off a little accumulated personal steam and the potentially dangerous, insane individual.

Sometimes a body can get so worked up about an issue that he sounds perfectly batty when he puts his ideas and feelings down on paper. This does not necessarily make him so, however. It's up to us to separate the righteous wheat from the wild-eyed chaff, to mix a metaphor. Thus we undertake all our investigations with such a light hand, such a clear lack of anything approaching the authoritarian, that we have never made a serious gaff yet or even gotten anybody's back up very far.

Certain groups other than those I've mentioned are also kept under scrutiny by the Secret Service. One of these is made up of people who seek out the company of the famous—without an invitation to do so. The chances are that these gate-crashers are harmless, but, as I've said, I took no chances.

For example, there are the two brothers; these "fun-loving" pranksters are identical twins and are quite handsome and intelligent-looking. They delight in crashing VIP gatherings and causing a disturbance. Their "act" is not always unfunny.

For instance, one of them, not long ago, made a public nuisance of himself. The police were called and during the ensuing wait the culprit disappeared. Just as the officer arrived on the scene the culprit's twin brother, dressed in the same clothing, made his appearance. Many people identified him as the offender. The officer arrested him and he went along meekly—one might almost say eagerly. When he was booked he called his lawyer and sued the police department. For what? False arrest of course, and he had an unbreakable case.

The twins like to get into highly secret, almost sacrosanct areas, say a quite high-priority section of the Pentagon and there engage in a wild, screaming free-for-all fight, pushing over filing cabinets, throwing furniture and generally raising Cain. The shocked inhabitants, used to the ultimate in protected quiet, look on such a spectacle appalled. Suddenly the two wildly furious antagonists will stop fighting and make up; then, sweetly smiling at the crowd that has collected, they will disappear, arms over each other's shoulders, leaving others to clear away the debris.

On one occasion they entered an airplane in which a well-known general was traveling. They waited till they had their opportunity and then went up to the officer and made a citizen's arrest of him. They claimed he'd been spitting on the floor or some such nonsense and that they wanted him imprisoned at once. The general was naturally highly indignant but nobody on the plane, when it came right down to it, knew enough law to stop this travesty. Actually a citizen's arrest is perfectly legal. The general won the day by standing his ground till the plane was ready to take off and the twins, who had no passage, had to leave.

These two men are probably quite harmless. But one of their pranks could become unintentionally dangerous. We keep our eye on them just in case.

Somewhat less safe from the standpoint of potential emotional crack-up are certain chronic and less cheerful gate-crashers. These people are pure and simple exhibitionists and some have very definite psychological problems. We know of a number of these individuals and we have them completely ticketed. There are no lengths to which they will not go to get into places where the famous foregather. And they are ingenious.

One of them repeatedly broke through the Russian guard maintained around Khrushchev when he visited Iowa in 1959, and became a bothersome nuisance. Another uses every gate-crashing technique in the book. I don't know how he does it sometimes, but he has gotten very important people to vouch for his presence at big occasions. At the last Democratic and Republican Conventions, however, he failed to find such a sponsor and so he forged documents which purported to prove he was a representative of a large Canadian TV company.

This poseur got into both conventions. Before we spotted him on these occasions he had joined up with high-ranking people as they stood around. He'd laugh and talk with them as though he were one of them, then he would hand a small camera to a member of the group and ask him to take his picture with the most important person present. As I recall, he even got a picture of himself with his arm around Mr. Nixon.

Are these gate-crashers potentially dangerous? Conceivably. We have sought the counsel of psychiatrists on this type of personality. They agree that such actions could be indicative of a serious underlying problem which could come to the surface and cause trouble. So we keep them all under surveillance.

Still, these particular people, the pranksters and the gate-crashers, are comparatively innocuous. There are other members of the lunatic fringe in this country who we feel are potential sources of more serious danger. They include a profusion of rabble-rousing individuals and demagogic societies. This section of the lunatic fringe has such a variety of representatives that I am going to pick only two to illustrate how dangerous they are.

Let us first look at a former general in the Army who's been involved in many odd escapades. His latest gambit has been to incite the American Indian to a condition of self-pitying frenzy.

Here is what he did. He told the Indians that the United States was still at war with them; that no final peace treaty had ever been signed between the Indian nations and this country. This meant, he said, that our government had no jurisdiction over the Indians, nothing to say about their lands or their rights. He convinced them that their leaders should go to Washington to have a powwow with Big Chief President.

And they did just that, one hundred of them. They came to Washington and did a war dance in front of the White House. They demanded that the President give them money for the lands we had "stolen" from them. They demanded also that the President recognize them as a sovereign nation and deal with them through proper diplomatic channels, sending our ambassador and receiving theirs.

I had to reinforce our guard at the White House fence, for in such instances we must be prepared for an attempt to rush the gates. But of course our real concern was that some of the more disturbed members might take some kind of insane action on their own. We are not afraid of political viewpoints, only what emotionally upset people will do with such viewpoints.

Actually, this particular individual is fascinating, in an offbeat way. He really is a general in the army. He was retired for a physical disability following a medical diagnosis of "psychoneurosis, reactive depression (situational), mild." Since then he has raised unmerry hell all over. Perhaps his most ambitious endeavor was the founding of the Minute Men For The Constitution, an organization that stirred up anti-Catholic sentiment. Here is one of his written contributions to peace and good will among men.

The "Brass" of the Pentagon is so steeped in the philosophy of violence promoted by Big Money and Pius XII, and is so indoctrinated in blind, unthinking obedience, that it has long ago surrendered all sense of obligation under the oath to defend the Constitution.

And another typical pearl:

It [Roman Catholicism] backed Hitler, Mussolini, and Japan against the United States during World War II. Roman Catholicism was involved in the assassination of Abraham Lincoln and every other of our assassinated Presidents.

Men of this stamp do not themselves cause us concern. It is their more demented followers we must identify and guard against. For, in a frenzy brought on by one of their leaders' blasts of hate, these weak-minded individuals might well take it upon themselves to straighten matters out in their own insane way, perhaps with a bullet aimed at the President.

But the aforementioned individual is only the mildest source of discomfort to me in contrast to my feelings when I contemplate a group called the NOI. The initials stand for the Nation of Islam. It is sometimes referred to as "The Muslims," and its membership in this country may be as high as seventy thousand, with active organizations in over twenty large cities.

This group, whose membership is entirely colored, attempts to arouse violent feelings of racism. It trains its men as soldiers and instructs its young men and women in an odd and distorted form of Mohammedanism.

The NOI teaches its members that the Black Race (its own term) was the original race on earth and that other races are offshoots from it. Its leaders claim that the White Race or "Devil Race" enslaved the Black Race and never allowed it to learn its real identity or history. All this happened because Allah was obliged to punish the Black Race for some vague crime it had once committed and would not let it find out about itself for a specified number of aeons. Now, however, the allotted time for punishment is running out.

With this Pandoran set of premises the NOI carries out a constant indoctrination of its members with anti-White, anti-Christian Church and anti-United States Government propaganda. Its message has been accepted wholeheartedly by its followers, who even change their names because they do not wish to bear the "slave" names given to them by their White Devil masters.

An additionally disconcerting item: NOI's leader, Elijah Muhammad (a Negro born in Georgia in 1897), was given an IQ test while serving a prison term at the Federal Correctional Institute at Milan, Michigan, in 1943. His score was 70 to 79—considerably below average.

I feel that there is something peculiarly sinister about a rabble which can be led by such a person. The incredible, blundering, bloody harvest it could reap, in pursuit of its idiot ends!

We must keep a vigilant eye on this fanatic group. Many of its members might be capable of attacking our President, even were they not inflamed by such political nonsense. Encouraged to violence, they are potent sources of unthinkable mischief.

Here, then, I have given a picture of those the Secret Service fears, the people against whom it must continually be on its guard. As I review our elaborate precautions you will understand what motivates our constant watchfulness and our attention to the smallest detail.

c h a p t e r   6

Guarding a Very Social Man

WE HAVE BEEN THROUGH A LITTLE BIT OF ONE
inauguration and a large part of another and thus seen some
of the elaborate precautions the Secret Service must take when
the President goes out in public on festive and state occasions.
I'd like now to give a close-up view of the day-to-day life of
the Secret Service with Mr. Truman and incidentally show
how a President's personality can create very special dangers
against which I had to keep on the constant alert.

But first a word about the White House Detail, which one
always sees in close-up pictures of the President.

As I've mentioned, this extraordinary unit is forty men strong. It is responsible for guarding the President around the clock every day of the year.

The men in it are completely unique. For one thing, they all make an excellent appearance. They are also, on the whole, young, even if some are now getting to be veterans in harness. They are college graduates or better and come from various fields, though I usually liked them to have a background in some form of investigative work.

They are trained to cultivate a sober, relaxed appearance in public, for to be effective they must be as inconspicuous as possible. Nobody should ever be deceived by their casual appearance, however. They keep in the very pink of condition, are experts in judo, boxing and wrestling and there is nothing about firearms which they don't know. They are also crack swimmers, and are expert at fire fighting, horseback riding, landing a helicopter, handling a sailboat or speedboat, and keeping back crowds without irritating them, to mention just a few of their accomplishments.

A basic group of these men is always with the President whether he is at home or away from home. It is from the White House Detail that I selected advance contingents to make security arrangements beforehand when the President had to go out in public or when he went abroad.

There is another attribute which each one of these men must have and without which all the rest of their accomplishments would be useless.

Everyone of them must be ready to place his own body between the President and any danger to him. They must be prepared, as part of their duty, to intercept a bullet, the cold steel of a knife or any other weapon with their own flesh. The individual bodies of the White House Detail are, in the last analysis, the final defense the Secret Service has against an attack on the person of the President. They are human shields.

The men of the White House Detail have never failed to perform their duty when called upon to do so. And they have been called upon often.

Of course I, as Chief, had to make the over-all plans and blueprints for the President's safety both in and out of the White House. The Detail would carry out these plans. However I had one master rule from which we never departed. This was that they must contact me by direct wire or short-wave radio the moment the President moved outside the White House. And they must keep in contact with me at brief prearranged intervals during these outside movements.

These contacts had to be in code to guard against interception. Thus all day long (since our Presidents tend to keep pretty much on the go) I'd get news of the President's whereabouts when I wasn't with him personally. My purpose in sticking to this arduous procedure was, of course, to guard against any chance that the President would be ambushed and cut off from protective reinforcements if necessary. Or in case any other emergency might arise which would require my personal attention.

As I became more familiar with my new duties I began to get fresh and sometimes exciting insights into the problems of Presidential protection. These (and other observations) I committed to a diary I started to keep when I became Chief. Here is an entry in my journal which sums up one simple but all-important aspect of Presidential protection, and one which I can't underscore too heavily:

The main protective problems of every President seem to stem from some important trait he has, physical or psychological. Main problems with FDR came from his disability; main problems about Truman come from his unbounded energy and his independent spirit, which make his movements unpredictable.

My observations were right on target. The problems of protecting FDR were largely created by his physical helplessness. A man who must be carried or pushed in a wheelchair in times of danger presents very special problems indeed.

Whenever FDR traveled, for example, the Secret Service had to have special ramps built for him wherever there were steps; this was done so that he could be moved speedily from his car or boat or plane to his destination. The ability to move swiftly, particularly in crowded areas, is a basic security principle, and with Roosevelt the chances of bogging down and thus becoming an easy "target" in a mob were great unless precautions against it were taken. A bevy of carpenters with saws, hammers, nails and wood was part of this great President's entourage whenever he traveled.

The Secret Service had also with FDR to be extra cautious about dangers from escaping gas or fire or an assassination attempt with either of these, while, say, the President was sleeping or otherwise out of his wheelchair. He could not have saved himself in such a situation for he could not move without his wheelchair, and I have been told by members of the White House Detail that, though he was a fearless man, Mr. Roosevelt was apprehensive about being trapped by fire.

The contrast between FDR's physical helplessness and Harry Truman's on-the-go pep and physical vitality illustrates my point perfectly—that a President's traits, physical and mental, shape the kind of protection we must give him.

One agent, who had been with FDR and was then assigned to Mr. Truman after Roosevelt's death, tells the following illuminating story.

FDR had been in the habit of rising relatively late in the morning and having a leisurely breakfast before he could possibly rouse himself to become any more than a routine security problem.

Truman, however, on his first day in office was up at 6 A.M. and ready for the prebreakfast walk that was to become so famous. The agent who told me the yarn was taking his ease in the Secret Service quarters at the White House when suddenly he got an "urgent-urgent" phone call from one of the White House Police: "The President's leaving the White House, through the southeast gate. There's only one agent with him. Hurry!"

The agent and another veteran of the White House Detail looked at each other in alarm. It was still almost dark out. What in hell was the President . . . ? They patted their holsters and took off at a dead run.

Truman was already way up Pennsylvania Avenue with only one Secret Service man behind him—a situation without precedent in recent Secret Service history, for we always saw to it that a minimum of four men accompanied the President whenever he was outside the White House. Even as they pounded after him he turned down Fifteenth Street with that fast, easy-moving stride of his and was out of their sight again.

They finally caught up with him, having run well over a half-mile to do so. He turned his head and viewed them, puffing like steam engines as they were, and then gave them his famous grin.

"Mornin', gentlemen," he beamed, without missing a stride. "Nice day, isn't it?" He resumed his forward gaze. "Nice of you to join me," he added.

Americans loved the idea that their President was an early riser and that he liked to take a walk before breakfast. As the agent who told the story remarked afterward, "I knew that morning that we had a whole new set of problems to solve that we hadn't had to face before."

I personally have nothing against early rising and I am a tremendous admirer of Harry Truman, as a man and as a President, but I will say that his preprandial walks, innocent as they appeared to be, were potentially very dangerous from the security standpoint. Indeed, they were considerably more dangerous than President Eisenhower's golf games. Here are the reasons why.

The walks took place in exposed sections of a great city; they were usually over the same route; and they occurred at almost the same time every day. They represented the kind of "habit" that was hand-picked for the assassin.

Walking along a street, usually deserted at such an hour in the morning, made Mr. Truman a slow-moving target, the delight of a sharpshooter. A rifle with a telescopic sight slipped unobtrusively out of any of a thousand windows along the route, with plenty of time to aim carefully, and we would have been helpless to protect our charge. Or a fast-moving car coming suddenly out of a side street and swooping down on the President and his entourage was another possible method of attack; if such attackers carried a submachine gun and blazed at us as they came abreast, we would have had little chance.

I could not, of course, against the latter contingency, arm my men with tommy guns in public. Believe me, I thought of it often enough and I wished we could carry such guns. We later did while protecting Mr. Eisenhower on the golf links since we could then conceal our weapons in golf bags.

But there was no way we could hide them while walking with Mr. Truman. The point is, of course, that if we had carried them in plain sight the publicity that would have certainly resulted would have been a disaster. We would have looked like the bodyguard of some cheap gangster, or of a dictator. But the whole discussion is academic anyhow, for Mr. Truman wouldn't have allowed it even if I had taken leave of my senses and attempted it. We were stuck with only the side arms under our coats.

Mr. Truman himself, as most Presidents are at first, was faintly puzzled and a little amused at the constant, day-in, day-out, presence of his Secret Service guard. He was always courteous and co-operative of course; I have never met a man more gentlemanly in his personal dealings. But, as with so many physically fearless men, anxiety about what might happen in the future seemed childish to him, perhaps even womanish. Sometimes he would look at his ever-present guard with a kind of detached amusement and occasionally he would make a remark such as: "Well, do you think they'll try to rub us out today?" or: "You fellows make me feel like Al Capone. Don't look so intense, will you?"

[83]

In fact, Mr. Truman did not give up all evidence of believing the whole thing was a little ridiculous until the attack on his life by the two Puerto Ricans, Collazo and Torresola, outside of Blair House * in 1951. After that he seemed to realize just how necessary his permanent companions were.

I don't think Mr. Truman ever discovered the device I finally decided to use to guard against sudden attack on him while he was walking. It was a simple enough idea but I put it into operation with some apprehension. I had an automobile follow him, keeping just out of his view; the agents in the car had the proper weapons, the ones I felt necessary—telescopic rifles and tommy guns. These men were instructed to keep on the constant alert for snipers and for a sudden attack on the President by another vehicle. My only fear was that Mr. Truman would notice his outrider and veto the whole thing but, in this case at least, his brisk, eyes-front carriage during his morning constitutional kept him from any idle curiosity about what went on to the rear.

Still, I never fully relaxed about those walks. And as the publicity about them grew I liked them even less.

Newspapermen and the President's cronies in time took to joining the procession. Finally the "Truman Early Risers Walking Society" was formed—its originator was one Tony Vaccaro, who dubbed himself "Chief Follower." He issued special cards to an exclusive group, largely newspapermen, and it became a mark of distinction to become a member. Such hijinks made fine newspaper copy of course—and the

* Mr. Truman and his family lived at Blair House for most of his seven years in office. During this period the White House was being repaired and so I intend to take up the special problems of protecting the President in the White House later.

President loved the whole thing. I could never work up more than a hollow laugh at such whimsical goings-on, for each one that reached the newspapers seemed like an engraved invitation to the lunatic fringe to take a potshot at my distinguished charge.

Lest I seem overzealous, a gloomy Gus, or a hand-wringing prophet of doom, I'd like to point out that an attempt finally was made on the life of this beloved President. And the two would-be assassins opened their attack on Pennsylvania Avenue at the doorway to Blair House, the exact spot the President left every morning for his walk. There is evidence that the attackers at one point may have been tempted by newspaper accounts of the President's walks to strike in the early morning. Had they done so, their chances of killing our President would have been very much greater, for these two mentally deranged men were truly fanatic and perfectly willing, even desirous, of dying as martyrs for their "cause."

The thesis of the foregoing is that Truman's very vitality created the kind of protective problems the Secret Service had to face during his administrations. If anyone doubts this, here is a little story about this energy I take from my journal, dated March 12, 1949.

The President rose that morning at 6:30 A.M. and spent a grueling twelve-hour day at the White House. At 6:30 that evening he went to the Senate and picked up Attorney General Howard McGrath. They went to Mr. McGrath's home for dinner, where they were joined by Stuart Symington and the Secretary of the Treasury, among others. The President played cards till ten minutes to four in the morning. The Secret Service drove him home and he arrived at Blair House at exactly 4 A.M. Let's say it took him fifteen minutes to prepare for and get into bed. That would make it 4:15. He woke at 6:30, with just over two hours' sleep, and put in a fourteen hour day. And he was then sixty-five years old.

In addition to his enormous energy Harry Truman had, more than any President I've known, the common touch. The men in the Presidential guard who were with him day and night, year in and year out, loved him. There is no other word for it.

One of my most trusted agents, who has been with the Secret Service since 1941 and who has known Roosevelt, Truman and Eisenhower very close up indeed, feels that one would have to go back to Lincoln to find Truman's equal as a person. Many of my men on the White House Detail still speak of President Truman with real emotion, of his unfailing kindness and generosity. They identify with him, feel as if he were one of them. A veteran of the White House Detail recently said to me: "He didn't know what was coming when Roosevelt died. He was thrown into office. It might've been you or me. But maybe *we* would've changed. It hasn't changed *him* a bit."

Yes, he was one of the common people and happiest when he was among them. During his walks he'd often ask one of the Presidential guard to come up and walk alongside of him. His chitchat was of the most commonplace, even as yours and mine—how you were, how your family was, the weather, the state of the nation. He preferred to call everybody by his first name and seemed uncomfortable if he couldn't.

Floyd Boring, one of my top men on the White House Detail, tells of his reaction to Harry Truman when he first met him. It is so typical of the way most men responded that I am putting this in Floyd's own words.

"I'll never forget the first time I was introduced to him by my chief on the Detail," Floyd said. "Truman could have been your uncle or your own father. I was to chauffeur him temporarily. He shook hands with me and said he was glad to meet me and I recall wondering whether he could possibly be a little shy. He seemed that way. Well, we were alone in the car and I drove him for several minutes. Then he said, as if he'd been saving the question up: 'What's your first name?'

" 'Floyd, sir,' I answered.

"Five minutes more went by. Then he cleared his throat and spoke heartily, as if he'd just got his courage up, 'I wonder if you'd mind if I call you Floyd,' he said.

"It tore your heart out. You couldn't do enough for a man like that. Imagine, President of the United States and that humble and ordinary with his temporary chauffeur. That's greatness to me."

But Truman's humanity, his folksiness, were not an unalloyed blessing to the men who were responsible for his safety. Indeed, these lovable traits caused problems just as his boundless energy did.

For example: It is a cardinal principle of Presidential protection never to allow the President to stop his car in a crowd if it can possibly be avoided. Even a friendly crowd can, and often does, get out of hand in a second. And when it does it is a hydra-headed, idiot juggernaut pressing on its adored object in a manic frenzy. It could crush him to death and trample him underfoot in its blind love.

But Harry Truman was a glad-handing caution. My wife

[87]

calls him "cute" and I suppose that word sort of fits him. Because of his humanity and warmth he had hundreds of friends all over the country. And whenever he saw one an overwhelming desire for a reunion with that particular friend swelled in his breast and must be gratified at once regardless of consequences.

It never mattered where he was. He would stop highly organized parades all over this fair land and, while thousands cheered and the men of the Secret Service worried and fretted helplessly, their eyes darting hither and yon in the great crowds that always greeted Truman when he traveled, he would clasp the hands of friends dear to him and hold public and sometimes lengthy spontaneous conclaves with them, chatting about mutual experiences, people they knew and all the other things that old chums who have been separated talk about.

This deep attribute was the one, of course, most responsible for the defeat of Thomas E. Dewey, Truman's opponent in the 1948 elections. The trait licked me too, though for different reasons—and much as I admired it.

On one occasion, in Boston, the crowd had pressed in very close to the Presidential autocade and was making it difficult for the car to gain headway. I came back from my lead car on foot to see what could be done to hasten our progress. I was a little concerned about the crush around us. Just as I got to the President's automobile, which was traveling at about two miles an hour, Mr. Truman espied an old crony among the mass of faces. I saw the recognition spread over his face, followed by the upsurging "reunion" look, a kind of glazed, happy, "there's muh old pal Joe" expression that made his ear-to-ear smile almost incandescent. At the very next instant he caught my eye as I peered in at him through the window.

Now the Chief of the Secret Service is legally empowered to countermand a decision made by *anybody* in this country if it might endanger the life or limb of the Chief Executive. This means I could veto a decision of the President himself if I decided it would be dangerous not to. The President of course knew this fact.

At this moment in history Harry Truman looked at me and I looked at Harry Truman. He knew by my worried frown that I didn't like the closeness of the crowd. He felt that I might pull my authority on him right then, I am certain. For a moment the smile went from his face, as our looks clashed. Immediately, though, it lit up again in the radiant smile, the decided smile, of a man who must follow his inner promptings come what may.

"Stop the car!" said the President of the United States. He pulled down the window. "Hey, Joe," he called to his friend, "how are you, you old son of a gun. Come on, get in here with me."

Joe complied with alacrity and delight. Needless to say, my countermand died on my lips; I disengaged from this battle of wills. Harry Truman, in the grip of a friendly feeling toward a crony, was too formidable an antagonist for me, perhaps for anybody. At such moments I could become philosophical. If death must come to this great President, at what better moment than during an ecstatic reunion?

There were times, however, when his friendliness and compliance did get him into serious potential trouble and I had to step in. Here is one occasion that gave me several bad moments.

It happened in Newark, New Jersey, during a political campaign. The Secret Service had, as always, made a minute-by-minute advance plan for the President's safety during his visit. The Newark politicians wanted him and Mrs. Truman to parade after dark in open autos. I was against this but yielded to the political needs, as I often had to do.

For the parade fireworks were hung on strings over the streets and these were to be set off in each block several minutes before the President's car arrived. As I said, these festive arrangements had all been carefully looked into beforehand by our advance men and checked out as safe.

Now, however, I double-checked on the arrangements for setting off the fireworks. I knew from previous experiences that overhead fireworks could present certain very concrete dangers. I was solemnly reassured by the politicians in charge that their setting off would indeed precede the arrival of the open automobiles carrying the President and the First Lady.

But the promise was not kept. In the very first block the fireworks were set off while the open car bearing Mr. Truman was passing directly underneath the string which held the firecrackers. Sparks showered down upon the President. Mrs. Truman's touring car was directly behind the President's. The sparks fell on her too, singeing her fur jacket and falling upon her hat.

I was furious! Mr. Truman out of the goodness and trustfulness of his nature was for continuing but this time I put my foot down. I had the entire parade stopped. And I refused to let the procession continue until the fireworks were set off a block in advance of our entourage as had been promised. The politicians in charge complied reluctantly. I can assure you that that parade was a very stop-and-go affair indeed, for I would bring it to a halt at every block and would not let it proceed until I personally checked on whether or not the fireworks had been set off. If they hadn't been I'd make everybody wait until they were. Only when I was certain would I allow the order to go forward to be given.

Fortunately, the President was as forgiving toward his obdurate Secret Service Chief as he was toward the offending politicians in charge of the parade. He grinned upon us both alike.

Naturally, not all of Mr. Truman's pleasant peccadilloes led to security problems. Many of them are just nice to recall. And naturally, too, some of the security problems that arose were purely fortuitous.

One thing I recall about him was that he was a man's man from start to finish. Scanning through my journal there are a score of little incidents that show his pleasure in male company and the pleasure other men took in his. It's well known that he was a great poker player and loved the game, though the stakes he played for were low indeed. It's not so well known that, when relaxing or on vacation, he loved to bet. He'd bet on anything. And he didn't seem to care which side he took.

I recall once he bet one of the Secret Service men on the Tulane–Notre Dame football game, allowing him to select either team. However, when he won he reminded the agent that the agent owed him, the President, twenty-five cents, the amount of the bet. And this was eminently fair, for my money.

When he vacationed at Key West his favorite bet with his cronies was on the weather or on the temperature of the water which his naval aide took for him every day with a special thermometer. And every day there was a bet.

My new job of protecting President Truman went swimmingly for almost the whole of the first year. I was beginning to congratulate myself on my good fortune when fate gave me a very bad scare and a lesson in the absolute necessity of keeping one's fingers crossed twenty-four hours each day—for safety needs just plain luck as well as planning to insure it. It happened on September 25.

On that date the President was to visit his home in Independence, Missouri. He went by plane, as usual, and the flight was typical. Among other agents flying with the President was Henry "Nick" Nicholson, a man who hated planes almost, but not quite, as much as he worshiped Harry Truman. Kidding and joking and good fun during the trip had been constant. At one point Truman, walking toward the cockpit in a determined manner as if to take over the flight, said: "You fellers better fasten your seat belts. I'm relieving the pilot now."

A little later, however, everybody was indeed fastening his seat belt with a vengeance. For, about one hundred miles out from the landing strip at Independence a motor conked out completely. The plane was in very real danger, and the life of our President and the other passengers for the next twenty minutes hung precariously in the balance. Nicholson was an ardent Catholic and always carried a rosary when he flew. He now took it out and prayed assiduously.

Truman was totally unruffled, as cool as the proverbial cu-

cumber. Finally the pilot, with consummate skill, put an end
to the ordeal, getting the crippled plane down without even a
jolt. On the ground the President clapped Agent Nicholson
on the back and said: "Relax, Nick. We made it."

Nick eyed the plane thoughtfully for a moment. "I don't
really know which is worse," he said morosely, "to be killed
or to be scared to death." Truman roared with laughter.

For my part I reviewed with agonizing particularity our
methods and formula for checking the President's plane before each trip. It was an airtight procedure. We couldn't have
been more careful or thorough, not possibly. The whole frightening incident was an accident of the purest ray serene. I
managed to forget it in a few days—or at least not dwell upon
it too much. And it never happened again.

Harry Truman gradually became very attached to the
Secret Service. He liked us as an organization and he became
very fond of particular individuals in it. To Mr. Truman such
fondness always means lifelong loyalty. His high regard for us,
I believe, is why he felt he could lean on us for especially
sensitive duties, some of which have remained top secret until
this moment.

One such quiet task had to do with Dwight Eisenhower
when he was still a general, head of NATO, and uncom-
mitted as to political party. As far as I know, he himself never
did find out what Truman did for him.

Mr. Truman's sense of responsibility was all-pervasive. Also,
he was a very great admirer of General Eisenhower. Thus
when a report came to him that Eisenhower's life had been
threatened the President called us in. The General had refused point-blank to accept any protection. But Truman was

not to be put off when he liked a man. Thus on his insistence the Secret Service of the United States protected General Eisenhower around the clock long before he was President. And he never found out that such protection was being given to him—at least not to my knowledge.

Such hidden protection really stretched our ingenuity to the utmost—but we were able to keep it hidden and yet effective. I cannot say any more, for much of this information is still confidential, but in my opinion the General's life was really in danger at this juncture and Mr. Truman was quite right in assigning us to this task.

Another man Truman profoundly admired and respected was James V. Forrestal. A few eccentricities in the behavior of this great Secretary of Defense were profoundly disturbing to the President. He asked me to check Forrestal's belief that he was being followed by "foreign-looking" men. It was difficult to believe that such a hard-headed man as the Defense Secretary had become a victim of perfervid fancies. He wasn't the type and I could not credit the idea. My first assumption was that if Mr. Forrestal thought he was being followed he probably *was* being.

We started with the butler at Mr. Forrestal's home. This butler was intensely loyal to Mr. Forrestal and at first would not admit anything was awry in the Secretary's household. But under a long and intensive questioning the infinitely pathetic story came out. Mr. Forrestal did indeed think he saw people following him; he imagined he saw strange men coming into his garage in broad daylight to tap his phone. He also had lapses in memory and had, during the previous weeks, become increasingly nervous and upset.

The butler at length told us that Mr. Forrestal had become so overly suspicious that whenever the front door was opened or the bell rang, he would go to the area and peer out secretly to see who was there. And only the week before, Mr. Forrestal had come into the kitchen while he, the butler, was there. The Defense Secretary was wearing his hat but no coat. He often, in recent weeks, would wear his hat around the house, apparently forgetting that he had it on, or that he had decided to go out. On this occasion he looked right at the butler and asked: "Where's my butler?" When the butler said, "I'm here, sir," Mr. Forrestal looked confused and could not remember what he had wanted.

What shocked me was the final discovery: Mr. Forrestal had made out his last will and testament and the servants had found it. On top of it were several sleeping tablets. And several phials of such tablets were found in his bedroom and bathroom. Had he been saving his doctor's prescriptions with the intention of collecting enough tablets for a lethal dose and then taking them all at once? I suspected, from all the evidence, that this was his purpose.

Hurriedly I sent my melancholy opinion to the President. I was convinced that the Secretary of Defense was having a total psychotic breakdown, and that this was characterized by suicidal features. I was tragically right. Mr. Forrestal was confined to a naval hospital and shortly thereafter took his own life despite the most careful precautions to prevent him from doing so. Perhaps it was for the best for in the end he suffered the most terrifying hallucinations and torturing delusions. I know for a fact that the President was devastated by this fine man's tragic end.

The same type of note but in a happier key: The President asked me to check on a complaint by Justice of the Supreme Court Felix Frankfurter. The eminent jurist believed that someone was going through his trash cans between 5 and 6 A.M. every Friday morning. He believed that this person was rifling through papers he, the Justice, had discarded, in an attempt perhaps to discover information about important matters coming up before the court. When I heard the trash can incidents happened on Friday mornings, that seemed a little too bizarre to make much sense.

There was, of course, nothing the least bit wrong with the Justice mentally, as his conduct indicated subsequently. I had to report, however, a failure to discover anything amiss in his rubbish department, despite our most determined efforts to uncover a culprit. Our failure, nonetheless, did not destroy the faith of the Justice in the Secret Service. In his book he has the kindest words for us, praising us for both the high quality of our work and our apparent lack of desire for publicity.

The protection of the President, as I've said, was a twenty-four-hour stint. No matter where I was or what other aspect of my job was clamoring for my attention, I still had to keep in constant and direct contact with him and the men I had assigned to him.

Even when he was preparing to leave Blair House for the White House only three hundred yards away I was informed before he left and after he arrived. When his journey was more extensive, say to a theatrical performance or to a baseball game, I directly supervised the advance work and, if humanly possible, went along to keep a direct watch on events.

I did not, however, at the beginning accompany him on his vacations to the Florida Keys, which he took about twice a year. While he was there I felt I could turn my full attention to the tremendous problems being caused by a great nation-wide rise in counterfeiting and an even greater upsurge in the theft of government checks and government bonds.

As days flowed into weeks, however, and weeks into months, I became tuckered out and I gave in to my wife's insistence that I should go along with the President and try to get a rest myself. This I did and despite one disturbing incident (which, happily, illustrates an earlier point I made about the White House Detail) I got a really fine rest and achieved a fresh perspective on things.

Harry Truman was a demon for work but he was just as efficient and intense about his resting—one of the secrets, I'm sure, of his health, energy and longevity. I emulated him on this trip, for the Little White House on the Keys was almost thoroughly insulated from the kind of danger I was supposed to protect him from and so I could relax.

I swam by day and lay on the beach and sunbathed, and at night I went to the special movies given for the President's guests. I was far more tired than I had known. Layer on layer of tension and fatigue fell away from me. I realized that if my job could be so taxing, the President's must be shatter-ing indeed.

The untoward incident I spoke of occurred during the sec-ond week. I don't believe the President ever knew a thing about it.

There was a roped-off bathing area where we swam. When-ever the President went into the water two Secret Service men accompanied him. One of them would always place himself between Mr. Truman and the open water on the remote chance that a shark or a barracuda should get into the swimming area.

On this occasion the agent in this position suddenly saw a large barracuda moving at an angle toward the President, who was standing in the water up to his waist facing the shore. The fish was only a matter of a few yards from Mr. Truman and so close to the agent that he dared not even raise his voice, not knowing whether this might cause the fish to attack. Swiftly and quietly the agent inserted himself between the killer-fish and Mr. Truman, ready to take the brunt of the attack. He then called softly to the President to leave the water.

The President did not hear him. Completely unaware of his potential danger, he had, by a stroke of luck, already started to move toward shore.

Now the fish was no more than three yards from the agent, just lying there in the water as if studying the situation. When the agent was sure Mr. Truman was ashore he started to back slowly away. Soon the fish was out of his sight and he turned and came ashore fast.

He was shaken by the experience but he reported it to nobody but me, as was proper. When he recovered his composure he said something I shall never forget. "You know, Chief, I'm glad this happened," he told me.

"Why?" I asked.

"I've always wondered," he said, "whether when the chips were down I would really put my own body between the

President and any attacker. I honestly never could be sure till now. It's a relief to know for certain what I'd do."

I knew what he meant.

For my part, I checked on the chances of a fish like this getting into our compound again. I found that the odds were so great against any harm coming to the President from this source that our present precautions were sufficient to rest easy about the matter. So I resumed resting easy.

chapter 7

... and His Family

THE SECRET SERVICE NOT ONLY PROTECTS THE
President; to this exacting job the law adds the duty of protecting his family as well. In the case of the Trumans this posed
special problems, for the family included a twenty-five-year-
old, career-minded daughter who lived in New York City,
250 miles away from Washington, and an elderly sister who
lived some 1,100 miles away, in Independence, Missouri, and
who had a very marked penchant for traveling in automobiles
at high speeds.

Now I have a profound aversion to publicity. It offends me
somewhere deep in my police officer's soul. I don't even like
good publicity. And I must say I could sense publicity for the

Secret Service, a great deal of it, from Margaret and Mary Truman in the future. The law's the law for all that, however, and I set about planning for the safety of these two ladies with a will.

When Margaret Truman decided that to further her career she must have an apartment in New York the Secret Service had suggested the Carlyle, a conservative and handsome family hotel in New York's exclusive East Side Gold Coast area. Margaret fell in love with the place (indeed her father did, too, and still often stays there while visiting the city) and she selected a top-floor, three-and-a-half room apartment in it.

We checked that place as carefully as if the President himself were to stay there. We did a confidential run-down on every single guest on Margaret's floor and on the floor below. We went over the hotel from stem to stern and head to toe, checking it for fire hazards, elevator safety and putting its personnel through our toughest security wringer. Then we selected an around-the-clock guard for Margaret, seven men, two of whom were to be with her all the time. At night they were to station themselves outside her door after she retired.

Margaret Truman, who once said that as an only child she had been "spoiled" while growing up, had actually come to maturity as a very real person, easy, sociable, charming, truly mature. She was pale-complexioned, with an almost perfect skin, fine golden hair and a lovely smile. She was the soul of cordiality with the Secret Service men who guarded her and on five separate occasions she personally saw to it that they got raises. Such kindness made her later remarks about us in the press a little hard to take. She said we'd interfered with her personal life and probably prevented her from getting married while her father was President. We really liked Margaret, though, and completely forgave her those observations, for who knows what a strain it is for a person in her salad days, the days of her full youth, to have to endure an armed guard with her all the time, even outside her door at night, no matter how discreetly he may comport himself?

I supplied Margaret with three cars whenever she went on tour and this was often. The agents I had assigned guarded her carefully and faithfully, making advance arrangements for her housing and safety in the cities she was to sing in. You can gather how busy they were when I say that the estimate of Margaret's earnings in 1951 for stage, TV and radio appearances throughout the nation came close to six figures.

I also assigned a special three-man guard and a chauffeur-driven Secret Service car to Mary Truman, the President's sister. In addition to that I put a permanent guard on the comfortable Truman home on elm-lined North Delaware Street in Independence; sight-seers and thrill-seekers were not above entering this house and attempting to make off with souvenirs. It was, of course, still lived in by the President and Mrs. Truman whenever they returned to Independence, which they did quite often. To protect the privacy of the famous inhabitants I also ordered, at about this time, an addition to the fence around the house.

First intimations of trouble with "the family" soon came. As a matter of routine all my agents, whomever they were guarding, sent me daily written reports or, if an urgent problem arose, they would check with me by phone or by our special teletype system. The reports from the Mary Truman detail quickly indicated that she was a kind of minor speed demon. She would ask our agent-chauffeur to rev it up if he dropped below her desired minimum speed (only too often above the law's maximum, to put the matter gently). If the chauffeur seemed reluctant Miss Mary would try to coax him into compliance. Also, she loved to travel, I soon learned, and would take off for a distant destination at the drop of a road map.

The sweet uses of publicity often turn sour for the Secret Service and I knew for sure we were going to get a public scolding sooner or later from Mary Truman's antics. Don't misunderstand me. I really admired this elderly lady's get-up-and-go, and my hat was off to her then, and still is, for her display of Trumanesque energy and fun.

However, my intuitions about the end results of it all were partially justified when her car was hit by a bus in Kansas City. There were other near scrapes, but the matter really hit the wire services when she whipped our man Stanley up to an alleged seventy-five-mile-an-hour speed in Hopewell, New York. They were caught red-handed by a motorcycle cop. Now upstate New York is heavily Republican and that is simply no area for a Democratic President's sister to be caught breaking the law. The papers got hold of it and it was all over the place in no time.

TRUMAN'S SISTER PINCHED. SECRET SERVICE MAN AT WHEEL WHEN TRUMAN'S SISTER ARRESTED . . .
SHOULD WE PAY TAXES FOR A BODYGUARD FOR TRUMAN'S SISTER?

That's the kind of newspaper copy it made.

Then, seeing a good fire going, one Congressman promptly poured oil on the troubled flames. He denounced the whole thing on the floor of the House of Representatives, making new headlines and immortalizing the innocuous incident in the Congressional Record.

My phone didn't stop ringing for a week. You might have thought that I and the rest of the Service were a passel of interstate scofflaws who were out to endanger the lives and property of the American community on principle. It was very discouraging; years of faithful, effective service all counted lightly when weighed against this single trifling event.

The incident died down in time. It was nothing, however, to the front-page ruckus about the Secret Service that was stirred up when Margaret went to Europe.

I had presages of things to come in a trip Margaret took to France—though this didn't prove to be the main event.

On that occasion the French press had gone mad about the girl. The fact that Margaret was a serious creative artist and charming to boot whipped them up into a frenzy of Gallic enthusiasm, and the newsprint bubbled and flowed like shook-up champagne. From the standpoint of an agent, the chief danger on this trip came from the exploding flashbulbs of French news photographers.

But then Pierre, always one for the striking effect, went too far. Margaret, properly chaperoned, attended the Lido night club in Paris, a place most tourists go. A photographer took a picture of her which showed her looking at a typical French girlie show, that is, one in which the girls are nude from the waist up.

The agents guarding Margaret felt that the better part of

wisdom was to ask the photographer for the film. They were polite but firm and got the roll from the camera.

However this was, according to the fourth estate of the Third Republic, an insult to *"la Liberté Française,"* the integrity of the state, the rights of the French male and God knows what else. The papers blew mighty hot for a day and my phone was ringing every five minutes.

But this was only a dress rehearsal for what was coming, and it died down quickly. On a later trip, to Stockholm, the event that my prophetic soul had been waiting for took place with a vengeance. It didn't die down for months—and years afterward I still heard repercussions from it.

Now, as a preface, I must say that agents who are sent abroad are always men who have received the most thorough and specialized training the Secret Service gives. Part of that training concerns the very special attitudes and psychology a protective agent in a democracy must cultivate.

The bodyguards of the dictator may swagger, behave brutally, display their guns, be tough and ruthless. We, however, as a country do not represent or admire such qualities. That viewpoint was drummed into my men all during their Secret Service training. It was only when such an attitude had clearly become second nature with them that I allowed them to travel abroad. Above all, these "foreign service" agents are taught to be soft-spoken, unprovocative, diplomatic—never never never, they learn, may they shove anybody around anywhere.

Now here's what happened in Sweden. Margaret ("La Princesse Margaret des États-Unis," as the French papers had taken to calling her) went to visit the Town Hall in Stockholm. She requested that, while she was inside, no pictures be taken of her. The Secret Service agents protecting her remained outside the building and, while they were waiting, a photographer from a leading Swedish newspaper approached them and asked if Miss Truman would permit her picture to be taken.

One of the agents politely stated that she would prefer not to have one taken at the moment. The photographer then asked if there were any other photographers present inside the building and was told there were not—as there weren't.

And that was all there was to it. The above is not my version of the matter, either. These simple facts are the result of a special, urgent and secret investigation by the proper authorities immediately after the event happened, to determine whether official apologies should be made.

But, following this innocent contretemps, listen to some of the statements that came out, first in the Swedish newspapers and later everywhere.

Varied reports had it that the Secret Service agents had said, "If you take any pictures I'll knock you cold"; that the agent had shoved the cameraman; that two big agents had blocked the doorway of the Drottingham Palace Theater and would let nobody through while Margaret was inside.

Dagens Nyheter, Sweden's biggest daily and strongly pro-American, said in an editorial after the incident:

The pistol-packing American Secret Service man apparently accorded himself the authority to decide what persons would be allowed to enter a Swedish public building—what are the rules concerning the right of representatives of foreign nations' police forces to appear in Sweden? Let us hope the Swedish Foreign

Office informs the people concerned that there are limits for their competence in Sweden.

Aftonbladet, one of their leading newspapers, gave the most unnecessary and unkindest cut of all. "Miss Truman," it wrote, "is certainly in no danger here—after all, she is not going to sing here."

Some of the papers addressed themselves directly to or at Margaret. *Expressen* devoted nearly a whole page to the story and then pleaded: "Please, Margaret, ask Daddy back in Washington to recall the Big Bully who is at your heels. He is destroying what you yourself are building up."

And so it went. American newspapers, not knowing the facts, soon joined the chorus. My phone rang constantly now and letters were sent from all over the United States demanding to know if it could possibly be true that Americans were paying for a special bodyguard for Margaret Truman; did our men really carry their guns on foreign soil without permission from the foreign country's police department; were Margaret's traveling expenses paid by our government? This ambassadress of ill will and her armed retinue must be brought home at once!

In my opinion Margaret Truman was one of the finest good-will ambassadors we've *ever* sent abroad. The papers generally raved about her in foreign countries. She exuded charm and sweetness; she was the essence of "democratic" womanliness. Here are two typical headlines from papers in Finland, where she went immediately following the Stockholm incident:

"Public Bursts into Shouts for Margaret"—"Delightful, Ready-Witted Margaret Charms the Whole Capital."

An even stronger proof of Margaret's ambassadorial effectiveness came from the Communist press, although in an inverse manner. It claimed that Margaret's press reception was so good in Finland because "secret police prowling about Margaret Truman in Stockholm had already scared the men of Finland away by shooting at the Swedish photographer who barely got away with his life." (Shades of *1984!*)

This remarkable account concluded that "if Margaret Truman took Helsinki by storm it is the most successful attack which the United States has made on foreign soil in a long time."

Only hysteria caused by a refusal to accept just how fine an impression Margaret made could have led to such wild and irresponsible statements.

As I said, the repercussions from this affair seemed to go on endlessly. I was extremely busy with a multitude of Secret Service matters but the teacup storm over this tiny incident (or lack of incident, for nothing had, after all, happened) took up far too much of my time, rebutting, answering angry calls from members of Congress, receiving the press and what not. Gradually, however, it subsided to a strong wind, then to a light breeze.

The problems of guarding the Presidential family are always unique. Ticklish situations have a way of arising. Bess Truman was the soul of co-operation and she never occasioned me or the other agents a moment's concern. However, two of her three brothers, George and Fred Wallace, who lived in Independence, Missouri, sometimes gave me sticky moments. We weren't legally responsible for protecting them, but on certain occasions we'd "help out," or whatever expression one would use to describe our ministrations.

Fred Wallace had a way of simply disappearing and of not telling anybody where he was for an unconscionable length of time. Whenever this happened I'd be informed and would have to disengage a man or two to do some heavy sleuthing. Fred wasn't always easy to find for sometimes he'd end up in another city; we always did find him, however, holed up in a motel or someplace.

George Wallace was sufficiently steady-on domestically but, I fear, vocationally he was a Secret Service man *manqué*. He loved to review our security arrangements for the Truman home in Independence. And then come up with judicious criticisms of our work.

His suggestions varied; sometimes he would be for extending a fence we had erected, and sometimes he would come up with plans for remodeling the little ten-by-fifteen-foot guardhouse we had put up in the back yard so we could prevent busybodies from jumping the fence. I took his ex-cathedra judgments under serious advisement whenever I received them but they had an unhappy way of ending up in back sections of my files and I could never seem to lay my hands on them again.

Yes, the President's family was varied and various—as American families are and should be. And the President kept an eye, with the help of the Secret Service, on all of its members. Nothing could happen without Mr. Truman being informed.

I have rarely seen a man who cared so much about his entire family as President Truman did. My journal has many notes on the various members—from details of dizzy spells by Mary Truman while she cruised around the country to full reports on Margaret's doings.

We all admired Mr. Truman's concern for his family. When he was on vacation in Florida he would call Mrs. Truman at the White House every night promptly at six o'clock. Margaret would be connected from New York City on a three-way hookup. He never missed these calls.

Margaret came home from New York every weekend by train except when she was on tour. The President himself, with full Secret Service escort, always went to Union Station to pick her up. I never knew him to miss in this either—nor did I ever see his features fail to light up when he saw her coming toward him after a week's separation. The Trumans were indeed a tight-knit family.

And yet within this tight-knittedness they were individuals all. Their range extended from Mary Truman's wanderlust to Margaret's highly creative nature, Mrs. Truman's great inner dignity and kindness, and Mr. Truman's tremendous administrative gifts. The spread in their individual qualities is no more thoroughly demonstrated than it was by the attitude expressed by the President's mother on one occasion when she visited her son at the White House.

Mr. Truman had given a strong speech in favor of equal rights the day that his mother arrived. That night the President and his wife offered her the "Lincoln Bedroom" to stay in during her visit. "No," she is reputed to have said, "I will not sleep in that man's bedroom." Then she reflected. "Not, that is," she said, "until the North tells me what happened to the family silver during the Civil War."

chapter   8

The Joke

PRESBYTERIAN HOSPITAL
SAN JUAN, PUERTO RICO

DEAR FERDI,

. . . I can get a darn good job here. I am tempted to take it. It would be ideal except for the Puerto Ricans. They are without doubt, the dirtiest, laziest most degenerate and most thieving race of men ever to inhabit this earth.

It makes one sick to live on the same island with them. They are even worse than Italians. What this island needs is not improved public health but a tidal wave or something to totally exterminate the entire population. It might be inhabitable then.

I've done my best to hasten the extermination process by killing eight and transplanting cancer into several more. This latter hasn't yet resulted in any deaths. The matter of consideration for the patients' welfare plays no part here—as a matter of fact all

[*111*]

the doctors delight in the abuse and torture of these unfortunate subjects.

This horrifying letter was actually written in the early 1930's by a young American doctor who was doing research in Puerto Rico. It never reached its destination, if it had one. Instead it was published in Puerto Rican newspapers in 1932 and gave a tremendous impetus to the ground swell of anti-Yankee feeling there. A very thoroughgoing investigation by American authorities showed that the young doctor who wrote it did it solely for his own amusement. He had intended it to be a parody of the type of thinking, and the kind of thing said by anti-racist Americans. It was, the doctor held, a joke. Today we might call it a "sick joke."

There is a direct link between that joke and the terrible events that took place on November 1, 1950, some twenty years later, in front of Blair House, the Washington residence of the Truman family while the White House was undergoing alterations.

On that afternoon two men approached Blair House, loaded guns in their waist bands, intent on killing the President of the United States. These two men had, from the beginning, believed that the letter was no joke at all, but was perfectly serious, and described faithfully and accurately what American doctors did to sick Puerto Ricans. For one of the assassins, the man named Collazo, the words of the young doctor's letter were a torment which he could not eradicate from his mind. And the fact that the U.S. not only did not arrest and punish the doctor, but rather, indeed, exonerated him, was absolute proof to this mentally disturbed fanatic that Americans had an unspeakable contempt for the Puerto Rican people.

This famous assassination attempt illustrates such varied aspects of our Secret Service work that I do not feel it has been adequately described in the usual accounts. Indeed, the event is so many-faceted that I hardly know which aspect of it to emphasize first. Perhaps it would be best, then, to start with the actual attack.

The first thing I want to point out is the way the Presidential guard was disposed at the moment of attack. The position of the entire protective force was based on a principle I had worked out with the White House Detail and which I've touched on slightly before. I called this principle our "defense in depth"—and we maintained it around the President twenty-four hours a day.

In this case, since the President was at his residence, the outer ring, composed of White House policemen * and Secret Service agents belonging to the White House Detail, was stationed on the sidewalk in front of Blair House and covered all entrances, front, center and rear. This ring, being in public, wore side arms only.

The middle ring was stationed just inside the house and covered all stairways. This ring had side arms and, concealed in a separate hiding place easily available to them, tommy guns and other defensive weapons.

The inside ring was stationed immediately outside the President's door. The men of this portion of the guard depended on their side arms, but of course they had speedy access to the cache of high-powered weapons.

When I speak of this kind of defense, concentric and in

* I will go into the matter of this uniformed branch of the Secret Service later, when the Presidential family returns to its permanent quarters at the White House.

depth, I must point out that this does not mean that there are rings of human beings completely encircling the President. It is enough that the Presidential guard keeps every means of *approach* to the President under surveillance. The natural protection given by a series of three concentric walls in any building the President is in is considered sufficient for most purposes. We simply augment the protection of such walls by guarding their entrances. In a sense we are an extension of such walls, trying to enclose the Chief Executive completely within their safety.

When the attack came on that afternoon I was, unfortunately, not present. I had eaten a leisurely lunch and had finished so early that I'd decided to get a much needed haircut. At 2:15 P.M. I had gotten out of the barber chair. I stepped out of the shop and started to stroll back along Fifteenth Street N.W. (see diagram facing page 116) to my office in the Treasury Building. Suddenly I thought I heard shots but quickly decided the noise was caused by a car backfiring. Then I saw police cars and an ambulance going toward Blair House and I heard the noise of sirens. At this point I quickened my pace and then a man came past me running. I yelled to him, asking what had happened, and he slowed down and yelled: "Some government men have just shot two civilians outside Blair House." My heart did a double flip at this bizarre account and I took off at a run and arrived just as the melodramatic action finished. I took immediate charge of the situation, of course. Here is my own version of the attack on Mr. Truman as I was able to reconstruct it in the next several weeks.

At the very moment that I was leaving the barbershop the

two assassins were moving in on Blair House. They had strolled down and taken a look at the situation outside the Presidential residence shortly before. Then they had retired to the corner of Fifteenth Street and Pennsylvania Avenue. Here they had shaken hands and parted. They were never to meet again in this life and indeed both fully expected to die.

Torresola crossed Pennsylvania Avenue to the south side and walked slowly westward on it, passing the Treasury Building and the White House. According to the plan he was to pass Blair House on this side and then, about two hundred yards down the street, cross back to the north side of the avenue and come back toward the President's residence.

When they parted, Collazo stayed on the north side of Pennsylvania Avenue, the Blair House side, and simply strolled back toward that residence. He cut an odd figure as he trudged toward his fate, certain of death. He had bought himself a whole new outfit for the occasion. He had on a brand-new suit with gaudy chalk stripes. His brown shoes were highly polished, and sitting jauntily on his shiny black hair was a brown fedora. A red tie had been carefully selected to go with his blue shirt.

Collazo kept his eye, in this death march, glued to the movements of Torresola. Now he had to slow down his pace because his friend had the farther distance to go and their pincer movement must be timed perfectly. Finally, he saw Torresola recross Pennsylvania Avenue and start back toward Blair House.

Collazo quickened his pace.

On the outer perimeter of our defense, the sidewalk outside Blair House, the guards were totally unaware of what was happening. (They were stationed in guard booths at either end of the residence.) It is now time to meet the men who, in a few short seconds, were to face the two armed fanatics closing in on them.

Standing within the guard booth on the west was a man who was about to prove himself in a way that few men are called upon to do. His name was Leslie Coffelt, a member of the Secret Service's White House Police. Coffelt's station had to be passed by Torresola before the killer could get to the Blair House entrance.

Torresola now came up to this west booth. He looked through the glass window on one side and saw that Coffelt was inside. He approached the doorway of the little edifice, as if he were going to ask a question. Suddenly, however, he drew his gun. Coffelt was caught completely by surprise. Torresola held the gun against his own chest with both hands in order to doubly insure his marksmanship. Then he pulled the trigger.

Just before this, Collazo had come up to the east booth. Inside was another White House police officer, Joseph C. Davidson. He was talking to the agent in charge of the White House Detail for that day, Floyd M. Boring, one of my best men. Floyd was standing directly at the entrance to the booth chatting with Davidson.

Collazo sauntered past these two men, mixing inconspicuously with several pedestrians who were just then passing, and came to the steps leading to the entrance of Blair House. On guard here was Donald T. Birdzell, another White House policeman. He was half-turned away from Collazo and did not see him take a gun from his belt and point it directly at

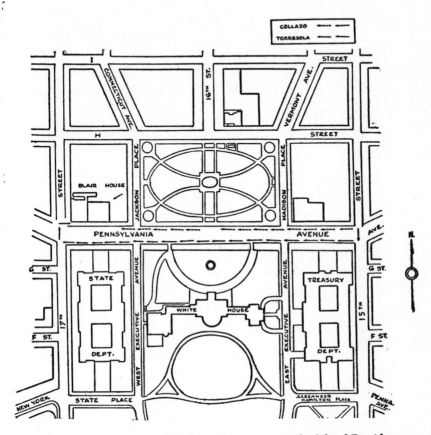

The routes of the two assassins in the attempt on the life of President Truman, November 1, 1950.

him. Collazo's finger squeezed down upon the trigger. It made a loud click but the gun did not go off. Birdzell turned, almost casually, only half-curiously, to see what had made that snapping sound.

Now for a moment let us leave this terrifying outdoor tableau and glance inside. President Truman was napping in the room just above this scene. It was a hot Indian summer day and he had stripped to his underwear and thrown himself down for what he called his "forty winks." He had had lunch and had retired for this short siesta at 2 o'clock, leaving a call for 2:30. Our President, in a few minutes, was to do a very foolish and dangerous thing—which might have cost him his life. At this moment, however, he was sound asleep.

Downstairs, a single guard watched over the front stairs which led to the President's bedroom. This was Secret Service Agent Stewart Stout. This man, during the heat of the onrushing melee, was to perform a deed which only those who have been in a similar situation will understand. To my mind, his act, simple as it may appear, was the very essence of courage, as heroic as anything that happened on that day of brave deeds.

What of the other inhabitants of this famous house at this moment? The domestic servants were circulating freely, doing their appointed tasks. Well out of harm's way in another section of the house, far from the shooting, were the First Lady and her mother, Mrs. David Wallace, who was ill. Margaret was off on a concert tour and had just reached New England.

Now let us return to the scene outside.

When Collazo had pointed his pistol at Officer Birdzell's

back and it had not gone off, the assassin looked at his gun in total astonishment. Then he started to pound it frantically with his other hand. That was the picture which greeted Birdzell when he turned his head to see what had caused the loud clicking noise. With the swiftness born of years of practice and of visualizing an episode like this, Birdzell took in the situation in a fractional instant and reached for his gun. But in that brief moment Collazo's hangfire discharged and the bullet hit the officer in the left knee.

Birdzell now did an enormously brave thing. To keep his own fire from wounding innocent bystanders, he whirled and dashed a few yards into Pennsylvania Avenue, his gun in hand, while Collazo continued to fire at him. Then the officer wheeled and, with nobody between him and Collazo, opened fire on that killer.

When Collazo saw Birdzell running he believed he had put him to rout. Now he turned and started to run up the steps of Blair House. At this instant the two men in the booth, Officer Davidson and Special Agent Boring, opened fire. Collazo turned and fired back. In a moment he discovered that his gun was empty.

It was at this point that Collazo did an astonishing thing—astonishing for its coolness. Amid the hail of bullets around him he calmly sat down on the steps of Blair House and reloaded his gun. His act may have saved his life, for an iron picket fence bordered the lawn and stairway and this protected him from the bullets. The whizzing pellets now smashed against the pickets and ricocheted off. He was hit twice, but my men could not aim because of the fence and the bullets just nicked his nostrils and his ears. However, when his gun was reloaded he stood up to fire again. He let loose with three more shots when, at last, he was hit in the chest himself and toppled over, his gun falling from his hand.

Collazo's marksmanship had, fortunately, been execrable. But let us turn to Torresola, for, tragically, his was brilliant.

If you recall, Torresola had cornered Private Coffelt in the west booth and, holding his gun against his own chest with both hands, had pulled the trigger. He fired three times, hitting Coffelt each time, and the officer went down. He was fatally wounded.

Seeing his first target fall, Torresola turned his gun on a man who was not on guard duty, but who was entering the Blair House west basement just as the killer had come up to the booth. This was White House Policeman Joseph H. Downs. Torresola fired three times and each time his bullet found its mark. Downs fell, critically wounded, unable to move.

Now Torresola tried to come to the rescue of the beleaguered Collazo. He ran onto the Blair House lawn. From there he fired one shot at Birdzell and once again his bullet found its mark; it hit Birdzell in his right knee. With both of his legs gone this officer fell helplessly to the ground and was unable to continue in the fray.

But now there occurred the final and bravest act of this terrifying encounter. Torresola, out of bullets, paused to reload his gun. He had left Officer Coffelt on the floor of the guardhouse mortally wounded. It seems incredible what Coffelt now did. Bleeding from three wounds, in great pain, and at the point of death, he pulled himself to the outside of the booth. With his last remaining strength he raised his gun, and,

[119]

leaning his arm against the side of the booth, he steadied himself. Then he fired.

The bullet hit Torresola in the head and entered his brain. A puzzled look came fleetingly to the assassin's face and it turned, in an instant, to a glazed, unseeing stare. He was dead before he reached the ground.

During all this the noise of the shooting had caused pandemonium inside Blair House. I have mentioned that one agent, Stewart Stout, performed valorously. What did he do? He held to his station despite the most overwhelming kind of moral pressure on him from those around him.

Stout was in the middle ring around the President, stationed at the front stairway leading to Mr. Truman's bedroom. When he heard the shooting outside he had at once gone to the secret place where the tommy guns were cached. Seizing one, he had taken his prearranged post on the stairway facing the front door. If Collazo or Torresola had been able to get through that door they would have been faced with a hail of bullets from this representative of our second line of defense.

The noise of the shooting, of course, alarmed the household staff inside. Some peered out the windows and they saw the awesome battle going on, with wounded White House policemen lying on the pavement bleeding. Not knowing Stout's secret instructions to hold his position inside no matter what happened outside, they wondered why he was not going to the rescue of his comrades.

Angry glances were directed at the armed figure of the agent. At last one person, a high-ranking member of the President's domestic staff, spoke for them all. "Your mates are being shot down," he yelled at Stout. "What's wrong with you? Go help them!"

But Stout would not be bullied or tempted. He would not yield to the invitation either to achieve glory or save his reputation for courage. To him his duty was clear. That was all there was to it. Stout's refusal to move from his post was equaled that day only by Coffelt's act of dying heroism. And it was a day of much bravery from all of my men.

Even before I arrived a crowd began to form quickly. And at this juncture President Truman, who had of course been awakened by the shooting, made his foolish move. Hearing no more shots he came to the window and peered down at the scene below. He was in full view of the crowd as he did so.

One of my men saw him. He waved his arms in alarm and called out: "Get back, get back." The President, collecting himself swiftly, obeyed.

What the agent who commanded the President to get back was afraid of was that the two Puerto Ricans, lying on the ground apparently dead, had other confederates. If there had been even one in the crowd that had gathered he would have had the shot at the President that Torresola and Collazo had been willing to die to get. And the course of modern American history might have been changed.

This latter kind of speculation raises the question of just how much chance the two would-be assassins had to bring off their mad coup. The matter is very difficult to assess.

Their scheme was a foolish one basically. Even insane people seem to know intuitively that their chances are improved considerably if they catch their quarry off guard. To storm a building surrounded by armed men is, on the face of it, fool-hardy.

However, the Puerto Rican killers had two very important things going for them. They had, and took full advantage of, the crucial element of surprise. And they were totally willing to die in their attempt to kill their man.

For a moment, at any rate, this tactical surprise swept everything before them. The rest of the speculation must be a series of "ifs." If Coffelt and Birdzell had been put out of the fight entirely at the first attack, either or both killers might have gotten inside. If President Truman had come out of his room upstairs to see what the disturbance was, they might have gotten a shot at him from below. Torresola was such a superior marksman that he might actually have outgunned Stout on the inside stairway.

Such speculations of course are idle. One thing is certain, however. The would-be killers could have had a much better shot at Truman an hour later. He was scheduled to speak at Arlington Cemetery then and, seated in the crowd, Torresola might have achieved his end.

I had much to do when I arrived. Men lay on the ground all about. Torresola was dead. Coffelt was unconscious and died a few hours later. Collazo also was unconscious and losing blood from a serious chest wound—I was certain he would die. The others were wounded seriously and needed immediate attention, though, fortunately, none was to die.

When I had taken care of the men I tried to talk President Truman out of going to Arlington Cemetery. Written statements taken from Torresola's body indicated he was the leader in this country of the terroristic Nationalist Party of Puerto

Rico, which had been responsible for many bombings and assassination attempts. I feared that the plot against our President might be more extensive than we knew, for often terrorists will send a second wave to the attack if the first fails. I was, however, overruled by the President, who was completely undaunted by this attempt on his life. All I could do was quadruple the guard that day, and I went along myself. There was no further trouble.

That very afternoon I launched an investigation that was to continue for months. Fortunately, Collazo's wounds turned out to be less serious than we had thought and he survived, allowing us to reconstruct the true facts behind this assassination attempt. We were able, through him, to piece together all that had led up to the attack. There was no doubt of Collazo's culpability and he did not try to cover it up in any way. In the end he was tried and convicted and sentenced to die. The President commuted his sentence, perhaps on the advice of the State Department, which was seeking to improve our relations with Puerto Rico.

Thus ended this tragic affair. Perhaps it would never have happened if the young doctor had never penned the "joke" that Collazo had taken so seriously so many years before.

chapter 9

Counterfeiting —
Now and Then

As you can see, protecting presidents is a twenty-four-hour-a-day, nerve-shattering task. Nevertheless, as Chief of the Secret Service, I had another twenty-four-hour-a-day job that required and got my full attention too, impossible as this would seem to be.

The latter job was the endless pursuit of the counterfeiter within this country and beyond its borders as well. In postwar America counterfeiting had increased enormously and I had to keep our fifty-nine branches on an overtime basis permanently. It was my job to plan and direct a ceaseless, nationwide war on an enemy that seemed never to diminish in numbers or in energy.

No holds and no techniques are barred in this constant war waged by the Secret Service. But before we go into our methods for catching the counterfeiter let us first look at some fascinating facts about the counterfeiter himself and his art.

In the first place, who is the counterfeiter? Does he differ basically from other criminals? Is there a counterfeiting type?

The fact seems to be that counterfeiting attracts every kind of crook there is, so that one cannot say there is a counterfeiting type as such, other than that he is a criminal. There is something about the idea of making one's very own money on one's very own printing press that inflames the mind of the criminal with a greed that will not be denied. Be he professional gunman or heistman, be he dope peddler, con man, smuggler or thief, he finds counterfeiting irresistible if he gets a chance to practice it. Somehow he feels that, in setting up his own mint, he is going to the heart of the matter. And so, from his standpoint, he is. His crimes, after all, are generally committed to gain money. Why not simply omit the crime part and make the money? There's a flaw in the logic to be sure, but then, a thoughtful recidivist might sigh wearily, a criminal's lot is certainly far from flawless anyhow.

When the criminal does take to counterfeiting, however, he generally performs in the way he is used to in his own branch of crime.

The professional gangster, coming from the highly organized rackets, will set his operation up like a business, with a manufacturer, wholesalers, distributors and a "market."

The loner, generally a second-story man or perhaps even a

pickpocket or thief, will try both to make and to pass his own product.

Hangers-on around criminals will usually be just the "passers" of a product made by others.

Gunmen, whatever their approach, will generally see to it that somebody gets shot.

The con man alone can be counted on to add to the gaiety of nations when he undertakes counterfeiting, and we will examine his most hilarious trick soon.

But I don't wish to give the impression that making phony money is confined either to the criminal class or to the modern world. Counterfeiting has fascinated all kinds of people from earliest times, chiefly rulers of countries who needed money to wage war. There have been intimations of the existence of counterfeiters in historical texts since the dawn of recorded history. However, the honor of being the first counterfeiter on record must go to Polycrates, the tyrant who ruled the famous island of Samos, in Greece, around 530 B.C. He coated lead coins with a thin layer of gold to eke out his supply of the precious stuff. Other big-name counterfeiters in history were Nero and Frederick the Great. And Napoleon set up an actual plant to counterfeit money for his campaign against the Russians.

Nevertheless, most of the important counterfeiting has been done by less well-known criminals—what one might refer to as the "little man" of the criminal classes. The penalties he has had to face for his vocation have been, throughout history, fearful indeed. In Rome under the Emperors, counterfeiters were burned alive. In Merrie England their hands were cut off and, later, when that failed to stop them, they were castrated. The dim view authorities took of counterfeiting was based on their inevitable realization that, uncontrolled, it could destroy the nation's currency and completely ruin its credit structure. It was, as a crime, on the same level, therefore, as high treason.

Our country offers the best possible examples of just how destructive counterfeiting can be. During the American Revolution the British destroyed our Provisional Government's currency by manufacturing huge quantities of the bills used by the Continental Congress—the notes called "Continentals." So thorough a job did the English do that the phrase "not worth a Continental" became a part of the language.

After the Revolutionary War had been won the fiscal system set up by our new nation was an invitation to the counterfeiter—and one which he accepted readily. From 1787 to 1862 so-called "state" banks issued a major part of our currency. These banks were nothing but private concerns which had been given charters to print money by the state in which they were located. Such "banks" designed their own notes and their officials signed them.

This was a counterfeiter's idea of heaven. The notes were easy to imitate and, besides, there were so many differing notes that few knew what all of them looked like. Even a poor imitation could go far before being discovered. The false-money men went wild. At one point, according to a calculation made just before the Civil War, there were some five thousand various counterfeits of the state bank issues. Millions of dollars of counterfeit flooded the nation.

The state banks themselves were often shady undertakings. According to one chronicler, ". . . any bail dodger could get a bank charter, print a wad of notes and then blow town. The key was to make your bank inaccessible because if a holder of a bank's note couldn't find his bank he couldn't demand payment. Such wildcat banks with nothing but a charter and a cellar printing shop, sprang up all over the country."

A source called *Bicknall's Counterfeit Detector*, published in 1839, summed up the national situation with these figures: 43 banks controlled by charlatans—their money, while legal, was worthless; 54 banks completely bankrupt, their currencies repudiated; successful and widespread counterfeits made of 254 state bank issues throughout the nation.

Finally, in 1862, with our currency nearly ruined by the counterfeiters, Lincoln decided that the only solution would be a federal currency. Since then the Federal Government has gradually assumed full charge of making all our negotiable notes and coins.

In 1865, three years after Lincoln made his first move to "nationalize" the currency, the Secret Service was founded— for the sole purpose of protecting the new currency from the counterfeiter. Since that time this protection has remained one of our major functions, others being added over the years.

The Secret Service, throughout its history, has had phenomenal success in catching the counterfeiter. Our batting average is up in the high .900's, and this is so because we have worked out unique and practically flawless techniques. Our methods have given us a better record, I am told, than that held by any other police agency in the world.

However, try as we will, we have not been able to eradicate counterfeiting entirely. The best we've been able to do is to control it—and sometimes even that has been hard to do. A graph of this crime in the nearly hundred years of our existence shows depressing peaks of great counterfeiting activity, followed by troughs so low that the optimist would swear the measure of the counterfeiter had at last been taken. Soon, however, the line starts wavering upward again. In my own administration it hit two fantastic highs—the year I took over and, after I'd succeeded in bringing that down, it swung up again in 1958.

The inevitable resurgence of counterfeiting is not hard to explain. One factor at the very center of the matter is the astonishing and chronic gullibility of the public. Let me illustrate with a few examples.

A farmer outside Camden, New Jersey, sold a peck of potatoes to a passing motorist who gave him a twenty-dollar bill. The farmer blithely changed it and gave the buyer nineteen dollars in change. Later, while counting his money he saw that he'd been hoaxed by "play" money, the kind you buy in the five and dime for your six-year-old, and not good enough even to fool him.

In Malden, Massachusetts, a garageman gave a customer change for a ten-dollar bill. The garageman did not find out it was a counterfeit he'd taken till he brought his money to the bank for deposit. And what a counterfeit it was! It had been drawn freehand in pencil on ruled notebook paper!

One might think this garageman and this farmer were two of the most heedless men in history—but one would be wrong. Such inattentiveness is the rule, not the exception, and the casebooks of the Secret Service can attest to that fact fully. Anybody, however, can check this statement using himself as a guinea pig—just notice the next time you have to change five or ten dollars what little attention you pay to the individual bills you get in change.

One counterfeiter gave us a great deal of trouble by basing his whole technique of "passing" his queer money on his knowledge of human heedlessness. He manufactured one-dollar bills—fairly good ones too. When he could do so with sufficient casualness he would ask a counterman whether he could give him a five for five ones.

Most countermen would oblige, accepting the ones he gave them with barely a glance. However, even if they had scrutinized them with minimal carefulness the chances of observing anything wrong were not high. For this grifter always saw to it that four of the five dollars were genuine. Also, he would only allow himself to pass a single dollar bill each time. In fact, he never carried more than one such counterfeit on him, so that if somebody did question him it would appear that the phony dollar had been handed to him by somebody else. He would simply ask the counterman for it back, saying he thought he knew who had given it to him and he would make him take it back. It took us a long time to trace this careful and methodical money-maker.

Anybody can become a counterfeiter if he means business, and this is far more true today than it was thirteen years ago when I took over as Chief. In those days a man had to be (or collaborate with) a master etcher or engraver, for the printing of the counterfeit had to be done from a plate which had an engraved or etched picture of the bill on it. Now, however, recent scientific advances in the graphic arts have made the master craftsman of yesteryear almost obsolete.

Today all the would-be counterfeiter needs is a decent

camera, a small offset printing press and a little secret practice and he can turn out very creditable money. Largely this is so because of a simplified process which makes the engraved plate unnecessary. For this simplified process the counterfeiter need only buy a new kind of chemically presensitized plate, and he can get such a plate in any store which carries printing supplies. Then he only has to make a photograph of the note he wishes to counterfeit and "develop" it on this plate. The plate has been so perfected, brought to such a condition of reproductive sensitivity, that if the counterfeiter then simply prints this image with a small up-to-date offset press he will get a really deceptive picture of our currency.

So unfortunately easy has this process become that counterfeiting is now a temptation to people who would not have even thought of it in years gone by. This is particularly true of people who get a small amount of know-how from working in small legitimate printing or engraving shops. The simplicity of turning out almost perfect reproductions of nearly anything will often make the minds of such minor craftsmen move naturally toward counterfeiting. What they do not know is their negligible chance of escaping the long arm of the Secret Service if they try. It is less than one per cent!

Counterfeiters of this ilk are of course the smallest of the small fry. We keep our eye on them but our chief problem is the large-scale operation. This is run by the big-time counterfeiter and it is he who makes us use every ounce of our ingenuity, know-how and, above all, patience in tracking him down. Let us take a look at this kind of big-time operation to see what I mean. I will pick one that is typical.

chapter **10**

A Big, Tough Case

ONE OF THESE LARGER COUNTERFEIT OPERATIONS
can best be compared, I feel, with a fire that has been burning
underground. It is long in preparation, the events leading to
it each hidden from view. But then, from several different
places smoke can be seen, and now flames, and suddenly it
becomes clear that a major conflagration is in progress.

I have picked, as an example of the large counterfeiting
operation, one that first peeped aboveground in Chicago. I
shall call this the Bundy Affair after the most notorious of
the criminals involved. Actually scores of criminals and hundreds of innocent citizens were finally involved in the case,
which, though not by any means the largest we've handled,

shows the infinite complications that follow in the wake of every major counterfeiting operation.

But let us start at the beginning—when the fire first began to show. A teller in the Bank of Chicago noticed the first bill. As his fingers flew through the stock of notes he was counting, some over-all impression of one of them caused him to stop and to examine it—perhaps it was the texture of the paper, perhaps it was a glimpse of some typical defect in the printing process he had been taught to look for. At any rate, the bill proved to be a counterfeit ten-dollar note and, as in the case of all counterfeits, it was immediately turned over to our Secret Service office in Chicago.

I was informed of the new bill's existence, and as a routine matter told the Chicago office to proceed with the investigation. My instructions launched an exacting and expert scrutiny of the bill. First it was checked against records. Was it a counterfeit that the Secret Service already knew about?

We have every known counterfeit that has ever existed in the United States on file. Thus discovering whether a bill has been put out by known counterfeiters has become for our experts a relatively simple matter of comparing the new note with the ones we have. The bill turned out to be a brand-new issue.

Now the receipt of a new counterfeit note always creates excitement in the Secret Service office where it appears—a tingle of apprehension and concern, because it means that some new and unknown person or group of persons is in competition with the government and that another problem of unknown dimensions and dangers lies ahead—immediately ahead.

Such new productions are always taken over by the special agent in charge of the branch of the Secret Service in the region where the counterfeit appeared. He and his assistants set out at once to "classify" it, locate flaws by which the public may be warned and, above all, to see if it will render up any clues to its manufacture.

In this case the new counterfeit was classified as a "fair" production, meaning that under average conditions of commerce the passer would have little difficulty in passing it. It also meant that the bill could be readily detected as counterfeit by a really alert money handler. Nothing on the note, however, indicated anything about who or where it had been manufactured. At first it seemed as if this note would have to be listed as a counterfeit "without a history," the designation we apply to notes which show up in commercial channels and on which we're unable to obtain any background.

However, the examination of the note continued. The Chicago office was stymied by the fact that while there was a watermark on the paper the note was printed on, only a tiny part of this watermark could be seen. It would take a larger section of the watermark to identify it with any paper manufacturer.

But the agents persevered. Day after day a team superimposed the partial watermark on samples of the hundreds of known watermarks used by paper manufacturers. This part of the hunt seemed endless and fruitless.

Another tack, however, yielded a tiny lead. A chemical analysis of the paper showed that it contained a certain dye which had come into general use by paper manufacturers only two years before. This seemed like a rather weak clue at the moment, but the agents rejoiced at having discovered anything at all to go on.

A quick investigation now showed there were three places in Chicago where paper containing this new dye could be purchased. The three paper concerns were very large ones. In a great city like Chicago there are thousands of legitimate uses for this type of paper and literally hundreds of legitimate printing and engraving concerns who used it. Unless one had a very large investigative staff indeed, logic might have counseled abandoning this unpromising clue.

Well, logic has its place in law enforcement but the Secret Service has become famous not by investigating only what seems logical, but by a thorough investigation of every lead, no matter how slim. This was no exception and our agents plunged into the task of checking sales from the three large paper wholesalers.

Slowly and slowly they went through mountains of sales slips. Nothing. This done they went through great hills of bills of lading. Nothing. This finished, they interviewed scores of paper salesmen. The interviews were a measure of desperation. They were undertaken only because no other paths were open to explore. And yet, as so often happened, this last-ditch investigation paid off.

A young salesman with a long memory recalled from his scores of customers a transaction he'd made with a letter-addressing concern which had not fallen into the usual sales pattern. The concern had phoned him and said they wanted to buy some 100 per cent cotton-fiber paper for two customers.

They were making the call as a favor for two men who had just bought a large commercial camera from them. The men, the salesman recalled, were from Tennessee.

Our agents immediately descended on the letter-addressing concern. Here they corroborated the salesman's story and also discovered that the camera was paid for in cash by one of the men.

This man had made an impression on the cashier at the letter-addressing establishment—by his method of discharging his debt. It seems he carried his money in small brown paper bags. When the time to pay for the camera had arrived he had removed these bags from various pockets in his pants and coat and counted out the correct amount. Then he'd folded the bags and put them back in his pockets. The impression this left on the cashier was indelible and it was to be of help later in the pursuit of the criminals.

For the moment, however, we encountered another blank wall. The two men had left an address in Memphis, Tennessee, but investigation by our agents there showed it was fictitious. Our Chicago office informed me of the status of their efforts and we all paused to consider the next step.

At this point a careful reader may ask: "Why exactly does the Secret Service go to all this trouble? It was only one ten-dollar bill."

The answer to the question is that when a note appears we are, generally, in a race against time. It is true that on a few occasions only one bill has made its appearance and has not been followed by others. But this is rare. One bill is usually the prelude to a deluge. Our optimum goal is to get to the counterfeiters before they can get their money into circulation. We can often do this—generally on the basis of tip-offs from the underworld. When we can't stop them beforehand, however, we try to keep the circulation of the money down to a minimum by catching them as fast as possible.

In this case the investigation described above was painfully slow, perforce; and it led to a cul-de-sac. Later the evidence uncovered would be invaluable in the courtroom, but for the present it brought us no closer to the makers of the queer money.

Now the counterfeit began to appear in many parts of the United States. And then this issue was followed by the appearance of three other counterfeit issues, two ten-dollar and one twenty-dollar notes, all having the characteristics of the first ten-dollar note and thus, clearly, the product of the same gang.

As week followed week the four issues began to flood the country. Thousands upon thousands of dollars were accepted by unwary merchants and even banks. Within a few months these bills had been passed in every one of the forty-eight states.

The little case that had started in Chicago had now become the number one concern of the counterfeiting section of the Secret Service.

At this point I immersed myself in the task of directing this case for, when the small conflagration becomes a great forest fire, our whole strategy shifts, and our over-all plans must have a national focus.

How did it spread in the first place? Well, in such cases the original counterfeiters have been able to turn out a vast quantity of their money (by my estimation possibly as high as one million dollars in this case). They now peddle this money to wholesalers, criminals who buy large sums of it to dispose of. The wholesalers in turn sell it to "passers" for a much higher price than they paid for it. These passers are either "loners" or small-time gangs. It is through the passers that the money gets into general circulation.

In this case the wholesalers, while they sold the greatest part of their counterfeit in the South, managed to furnish scores of passers with sizable quantities. In the next months a mounting toll of complaints from the victims rolled into Secret Service offices throughout the nation.

Our technique for pursuing the criminals now became very direct—and horribly arduous.

We ran down every single complaint. And there were hundreds and hundreds of them.

If I were to tell in detail the intermeshing tales, the sordid dramas, the scores of broken lives that emanated from these counterfeits it would require at least fifty books of the size of this one. Every counterfeit bill that was passed had its repercussions of pathos or tragedy. Most of them do not concern this story, for they don't bear directly upon the pursuit of the central criminals involved.

Yet I cannot help pausing to comment on the endless woes that come on the heels of a major counterfeiting attempt, particularly if we cannot stop it in time.

The small-time passers are, often enough, people who dwell for the most part on the right side of the law. Some personal or economic desperation forces them to try this "easy" way to obtain money. They and their families are destroyed when they are caught—and we almost always do catch them.

If such cases are pitiful, what about the completely innocent victims? Every loss has its drama and its harrowing consequences—the stricken look of fear on the faces of elderly pensioners when they learn that the ten-dollar or twenty-dollar bill (which has been carefully calculated to last until the next check) is no good and is taken from them; the bewildered dismay of the widowed mother who had budgeted down to the last dollar for groceries, the dentist, school supplies for the children; the wife of the young serviceman who may be halfway across the world and whose allotment check is keeping his family secure in his absence—these and many more. Each day Secret Service agents see the anguish brought about by the counterfeiter.

But to return to our case:

My assistants and I had gone through reams and reams of reports from our fifty-nine branches describing the arrests of small-time passers. We looked at every word of each report for possible clues but each case turned out to be a blind alley.

And then, when hundreds of possibilities had led nowhere, we struck pay dirt.

In May, six months after the first ten-dollar bill had been discovered in that Chicago bank, a passer was arrested in Little Rock, Arkansas. With very little encouragement he sang, loud and clear and the burden of his song led us to John W. Riadon, of Memphis, Tennessee, clearly one of the important wholesalers in the case. At least that was our conclusion after we had looked up his record and had held him under secret surveillance for several days.

Now I decided to send one of my very best agents, a truly great expert in the art of "roping," into Memphis. This man, with the aid of contacts in Tennessee's gangland, was able to obtain an introduction to Riadon—passing himself off as a bona fide gangster who wanted to buy a big sum of the queer.

It took the most skillful kind of work on the part of my undercover man, but, after a few weeks he had so completely ingratiated himself with Riadon that the gangster fell directly into our trap. He sold our agent $75,000 of the counterfeit. As the money exchanged hands we took Riadon into custody.

Riadon was the middle-sized fish. But he was our guide to the bigger ones. In an effort to save his own skin he too sang loudly (counterfeiters, thank heaven, are in their very best voice after an arrest) and his song led us to the two manufacturers who had originally bought the camera and the high-grade paper in Chicago. The names of these men were Fulcher and Byars, both fair-sized gangsters in the Tennessee underworld. We had them dead to rights. We could trace their crime from the beginning, and identify them fully by the men who had sold them the camera so many months before in Chicago. We closed in on them, capturing their printing press and their other paraphernalia.

Now we breathed a sigh of relief. But the sigh was premature!

When a manufacturing plant for counterfeit is captured, the bad money it was turning out usually stops appearing pretty quickly. In this case, however, there was no such sequel and to our surprise the money increased as the weeks rolled by.

We felt sick at heart at this development but stolidly we returned to the fray—for another six months.

Again scores of arrests were made of small-time passers—and again to no avail. And then, as almost always happens, we were able to pick up the right passer, the man who was getting his counterfeit from the central wholesaler.

Again there was the sordid attempt to save his skin by

squealing. This time however the pointed finger led directly to Mr. Big himself.

This was James D. Bundy, one of this country's top criminals, on the list of our most wanted mobsters. He had, it developed, been a moving spirit in the entire counterfeiting venture. And with consummate arrogance he had gone right on selling the counterfeit even after the men who had manufactured his goods had been arrested. The gall of this big-time hood made it particularly gratifying to catch him with the goods and bring him to justice. With his arrest the whole counterfeit conspiracy collapsed and very quickly these four issue of spurious money ceased to appear. All of the criminals were tried and convicted and sentenced to long jail terms.

A laborious and slow process came thus to a grinding halt. Had it, we must ask, been worth the enormous efforts, the huge number of arrests, the following of false leads—all the trouble, the heartache, the expense?

Of course.

The integrity of our currency had been preserved once again. For despite the great amount of passing that had gone on, still only one-third of the counterfeit money that had been actually made had been circulated.

But I would like to make one more point. This single case took over a year to solve. At the same time as we were working on this we were also working on twelve other "big" cases comparable in complexity—and one hundred and twelve more of varying sizes.

My point: The Secret Service man is, to say the least, certainly worth his hire.

Coin Makers and Con Men

AFTER THE FOREGOING GRIM TALE LET'S TURN TO a lighter vein. As much as I deplore counterfeiting I must confess that it has its funny moments. These are usually supplied by the lesser echelons in the criminal social scale.

One group, the lowest in the whole criminal hierarchy, are pure buffoons. These are the coin counterfeiters. They are so small-time that they can't even take themselves seriously. The quality of their humor is no greater than their art, as can be witnessed by this story that went the rounds of the coin counterfeiters recently (though it does show their absurdly abject attitude toward themselves and their craft):

FIRST COIN COUNTERFEITER: I placed four of my best nickels in the chicken sandwich slot over at the Automat and guess what came out?
SECOND COIN COUNTERFEITER: What?
FIRST COIN COUNTERFEITER: The manager.

The joke could have been prophetic for one simple fellow, for, at one point, an Automat actually did have a great spurt in the number of false coins put into its slots. The management told us about this and we sent one of our false-coin experts over to investigate.

"Any characteristics of this crime or the criminal you've been able to figure out?" our man asked the manager.

"Nope," the manager replied. "Just the nickname he's earned for himself."

"What's that?" our man asked.

"Cream Pie Charley," the manager said. "We call him that because he always eats a lot of our Boston cream pie."

A long wait in back of the cream pie receptacle by the agent was the result of this information. After eight hours of watching good healthy coins plunk into the slot at the rear, the agent was dizzy but unbowed and then, at long last, his vigilance was rewarded. Plunk, plunk, plunk, plunk, four nickels dropped down, their phoniness visible and audible and palpable to the practiced eye, ear and hand. Our man dashed out into the hall and nabbed the crook, a round-faced little fellow in a shabby coat with huge pockets in it. A quick frisk in the manager's office showed the passer was loaded to the scuppers with scores of counterfeit nickels, dimes, quarters and half-dollars and had as well over two hundred slugs on him. The loot was piled on top of the manager's desk and now the crook looked at it ruefully.

Then he breathed a sigh of relief. "I'm glad it's all over," he said, imitating a remark often used by men who have committed somewhat more sizable offenses. "This has been worse than workin'," he continued. "Why, that damned stuff is as heavy as lead. It's like luggin' furniture around, only worse. I had to eat all the time to keep up my strength. I've gained about thirty pounds since I started passin' them coins. Boy, never again."

Humor on a higher key comes when the gentle grafter, known nowadays as the con man, puts the counterfeiter's hat on. When he does he generally employs a gimmick known as "the green goods swindle."

To put it simply, the "green goods swindle" involves a money-making machine which the con man has personally rigged up or has had made and with which he tries to extract money from any ordinary citizen who has larceny in his heart. Such people the con men call "marks."

The case of Wilson Pittsford and his money-making machine illustrates the matter amply. Mr. Pittsford was a con man first and foremost. His "machine" was a handsome wooden box which, when opened, exposed to view an elaborate-looking engine. When turned on, this machine made an impressive display of whirring gears, ringing bells and flashing orange, green and purple lights.

Too, Mr. Pittsford carried a handsome leather kit. This contained "secret" chemicals for making counterfeit notes; rows of corked test tubes with villainous-looking fluids in them, orange, green and purple, perhaps to match the flashing lights. Between myself and the reader, however, I think it is only fair to say that these secret fluids were nothing more than orangeade and limeade and grapejuice.

The money-making machine was not entirely for show, however. If, as Mr. Pittsford did, one bleached a one-dollar bill (itself against the law) so that it was nothing but a piece of white oblong paper, put it into the machine so that it pressed tightly against a genuine twenty-dollar bill that had been properly treated chemically and then turned the machine on, the machine would generate the right amount of heat to make a fairly good imprint of the genuine bill on the bleached one. This made the con man a counterfeiter of course and brought us into the picture. But the performance was enough to stagger a larcenous mark and in the hands of a man like Pittsford it was a money-maker par excellence.

Mr. Pittsford's latest depredation took place in a small town in Illinois, not too long ago. A confederate had preceded him there and had set the whole thing up. The confederate was a man named Taxley, another old-time con man. Once in the village, Taxley rented a bar and grill and then proceeded to look over the situation. He finally selected a local lumberman as his first mark, a greedy-looking, gimlet-eyed fellow named Lucane.

Taxley played his hand very, very slowly. He flashed one-thousand-dollar bills in Lucane's presence (he had two left over from the last "green goods swindle" he and Pittsford had brought off). Taxley spoke of his holdings in South America, of his desire to invest money in something good here. Lucane gradually was overwhelmed. Here was a man much bigger than he was; he became an habitué of Taxley's Bar and

Grill, and when he had been brought to just the right softness for plucking, Taxley sent his message to Wilson Pittsford to arrive posthaste.

Pittsford appeared at Taxley's Bar and Grill now, and in the course of time he was introduced to Lucane. Taxley, of course, affected not to know his old confederate but to be enchanted by his worldly talk. Finally, and apparently with great naturalness, this talk turned to counterfeiting. And now, swearing them to great secrecy, Pittsford showed the two a twenty-dollar bill. They looked at it with polite interest. Pittsford said he had made it with his own machine, and that it was absolutely perfect. Nobody, not even a bank, could tell that it was a counterfeit. Lucane demurred. Try it, challenged Pittsford. Lucane took the bill to the local bank and they gave him change without a murmur. When he returned Lucane begged to be let in on this money-making racket. Taxley also feigned interest. The bill Lucane had changed was, of course, a perfectly genuine twenty.

Pittsford at first refused their request for a demonstration of his machine's powers but at last gave in gracefully. Now he sent Lucane to the bank with a hundred-dollar bill from his own pocket, requesting that he get it changed into five new twenties.

You see, he explained, you can only take one impression from any individual bill; it's that fresh ink off the top that does the trick. Therefore you need a new twenty-dollar bill for each one you manufacture. That part was essential to the hoax and Lucane didn't even question this absolutely false statement but hustled off to the bank to change Pittsford's one-hundred-dollar bill.

With the five twenties and Pittsford's magic machine the men went to a cabin Lucane owned in the woods about twenty miles from town. Here, while the two men watched, Pittsford transferred the face and back of a twenty-dollar bill onto a bleached-out single. They came out in reverse, of course, and Pittsford now said that he'd proceed to turn the reversed image around the right way. He put the bill back into the machine, turned a few dials and pretended to wait. During this wait he sent Lucane into the other room for something and while the mark was away Pittsford simply substituted a genuine twenty in the machine for the one with the reversed images. A few minutes after that Lucane returned from his errand in the other room. Pittsford then turned the machine off and had Lucane look inside.

The mark couldn't wait to get the perfect-looking new "counterfeit" to the bank. Again a bank teller changed it without a murmur. And now the bait was deep inside the lumberman. The next day he drew ten thousand dollars from the bank, all in twenty-dollar bills and begged Pittsford to double this money. Manfully Pittsford resisted the request but finally, out of pure liking for Lucane, he indicated, he gave in.

Once again Pittsford brought his machine to the cabin. Five hundred twenty-dollar bills were stacked up in front of him—all genuine. The con man started to work, with Lucane hovering around him like a bee around a flower. Taxley hadn't been able to come; he'd begged off at the last minute with a phony excuse, a bad cold. But Lucane hadn't been disconcerted a bit.

The process now starts and the back of one twenty-dollar bill is successfully reversed. Back the bill goes into the ma-

[147]

chine to get straightened around the right way, and as they wait Pittsford idly counts the one-dollar bills he is going to bleach out. He had contracted to supply the dollar bills himself. Suddenly the con man curses loud and long. "What's the matter?" asks Lucane. "I haven't brought enough one-dollar bills," Pittsford says, "and when I make the final bleach I want to put them all in and bleach them out together. We'll have to postpone this whole thing till I get the right amount of ones. We can come back tomorrow."

But Lucane will hear none of this. He insists on going through with the job today. He will drive into town, he says, and get the additional one-dollar bills himself. With apparent reluctance Pittsford says okay, but hurry up. When Lucane returns, Pittsford has fled.

Actually Pittsford and Taxley could have gotten away entirely. But greed made them their own best marks. While they had been hooking Lucane they could not resist trying to set up another mark in the same town. A date had been made with this new sucker-to-be for a demonstration following the Lucane affair. But this mark was not so easy and the Secret Service received a tip-off from him. We caught the two veteran con artists red-handed, just as Pittsford had finished reversing his second twenty-dollar bill. And we put them out of harm's way for a bit.

There are many versions of the green goods racket. Sometimes the con man will sell the machine to the mark rather than go to the elaborate lengths Pittsford and Taxley went to. That was the version of the "green goods swindle" used by one of the ranking counterfeiters of all time in this country, one Victor Lustig, who had taken to himself the title of "Count."

Lustig was a colorful personality, though a very great rascal. He operated for over twenty years and, though he was in the toils of the Secret Service often enough, he seemed to have as many criminal lives as a cat.

The Count, as he liked to be called, was a real Fancy Dan. His clothes came straight from the best London tailors and when not in the poky he went about in a chauffeur-driven limousine and gave the most elegant parties in his beautiful and tastefully decorated New York City apartment.

The Count literally loved the swindling racket, both its con man and counterfeiting aspects. He is reputed to have once said: "Everything turns gray when I don't have at least one mark on the horizon. Life then seems empty and depressing. I cannot understand honest men. They lead desperate lives, full of boredom."

The underworld, that shadowy realm of fact and fiction, seemed to admire the Count and cheered him on to ever wilder and zanier exploits. He was a counterfeiter par excellence and one year at least he set criminaldom to buzzing in earnest. He claimed that he'd invented a process for putting tiny silk threads, just like the ones used in our currency, into paper. This would have been a great discovery indeed for the counterfeiter; it is one of the most carefully guarded secrets of the Bureau of Printing and Engraving. As it turned out, after we'd had him under surveillance for some time we found, with relief, that this time the Count was merely boasting.

Of all his dodges, the Count liked his own special version of the "green goods swindle" best. As I said, he preferred to sell his machine outright to the mark once he'd hooked him, and he got amazing prices for it. I know of no occasion in which he did not ask for, and get, at least four thousand dollars for this little engine, which may have cost fifteen dollars to have built.

The Count's machine differed from that of Wilson Pittsford. It was simply a small, not very impressive-looking box with a crank on the side of it. In his demonstrations to the mark the Count would put several pieces of white paper each the size of a dollar bill in a pile in a container inside the machine. On top of this pile he would then place a genuine twenty-dollar bill. Then he'd let the box sit for several hours, perhaps overnight. When the time came he'd crank the machine several times in the mark's presence and out would come ten or fifteen twenty-dollar bills.

How did it work? The twenty-dollar bills had been concealed beforehand in a false bottom of the black box. Turning the crank would set a mechanism in motion that would carry the white paper to the false bottom and transport the twenty-dollar bills to the space formerly occupied by the white paper.

One of Count Lustig's greatest thrills, by his own account, was his experience with a Texas sheriff, perhaps the most ingenuous man of this or any other century.

Lustig had been arrested in this sheriff's bailiwick, on a charge of counterfeiting, and had been remanded to the sheriff's very own jail. While there he dazzled the sheriff with tales of high adventure and easy money and a description of the green goods machine that must have been classic for it so aroused the latent larceny in the sheriff that this weak vessel of the law begged for an opportunity to see the wondrous engine in action.

Lustig promised that he would do so if he were freed. The

next day the charges against Lustig were dismissed for lack of evidence and he and the excited sheriff repaired to Lustig's hotel. The thing was almost too easy. The law was completely convinced by the Count's demonstration.

The sheriff had, he now confided to the Count, twenty thousand dollars in negotiable bonds which belonged to the county. But what had he to worry about? He would simply borrow the money to buy the box from the Count and return the "loan" when he'd manufactured it with the machine. Wasn't that, he wanted to know, the strictest kind of logic?

Yes, said the Count, and he'd give him a bargain. He'd only charge eight thousand dollars for the machine.

The bonds were cashed, the deal consummated, and Lustig immediately disappeared.

The sheriff barely noted the Count's sudden withdrawal. With bated breath he bore his new machine to his office and sowed it with strips of white paper and one good twenty-dollar bill. Then he waited—the Count had advised a minimum of six hours, just enough time for him to get a running start on all pursuers. The hours dragged their slow lengths along and the sheriff paced impatiently. Finally, however, the time was up and the harvest could be reaped. He turned the crank a few times. Nothing happened. He checked his watch. Yes, the time was now. He turned the crank again. Nothing. Again and again and again. A look of dreadful surmise crossed his rugged features and wrinkled his narrow brow. Suddenly he wrenched the top of the machine off and looked inside. Alone in his office he faced the duplicity of man.

Naturally the sheriff swore vengeance. He made a vow with

himself that he'd seek the Count up and down the corridors of the world. He'd find him and he'd kill him.

He did not have long to look. Another con man a mere two weeks later tipped the sheriff that Count Lustig was living in style in Chicago in an elegant suite in a certain ultra-elegant hotel. The sheriff posted to that city, guns oiled and loaded, and rang the Count's bell. A butler answered and asked him to wait in the Louis Quinze anteroom. In a moment the Count appeared.

"I'm going to kill you, Lustig," the sheriff croaked and pulled his six-shooter.

"Wait," said the Count, holding up a beringed hand. "I didn't bilk you. You're the victim of a mistake. I was going to wire you this very day. I just found out I'd left an important gadget off that box. That's why it didn't work."

"Huh?" said the once-bitten limb of the law.

"Exactly," replied the Count. "The box couldn't possibly make those twenties without that piece on it. I'm terribly sorry. I'll show you what I mean."

And so another demonstration started and this time the Count sold the extra gadget for another eight thousand dollars. The sheriff departed for home a few hours later set to make his fortune in a very literal sense. A few days later he was arrested for peculation and the Count breathed more easily. "It worried me a little," he said. "If they hadn't gotten him for stealing those bonds he might have been harder for me to handle the third time."

Ave Atque Vale

PURSUIT OF CRIMINALS, HUMOROUS OR DEADLY
serious, and the protection of the President left me little time
for loafing. However, as I have come to review my past for
this book, I have noticed one thing. Though my memory re-
mains essentially clear for most of the events that occurred
during my stay in Washington, a certain vagueness hangs over
some of the doings of the latter part of the Truman Administration. I think that there must be a wishful element in this,
for there is pain in preparing to take leave of people whom
one has known and admired as profoundly as I admired the
Trumans—and the steps leading to the farewells one, perhaps,
may wish to forget, to obliterate.

Here is a sad (to me) little comment on yesteryear in my diary:

March 2, 1952. Margaret still on tour. Report this morning that she has sore throat. Reported it to H.T. He quite worried. Received his personal instructions to keep him fully informed as to the progress of the throat condition. Wants reports in morning and evening.

And here's another homely and touching note:

March 27, 1952. President terminated stay at Florida Keys one day before he'd planned. We brought him to White House at 6 P.M., very excited at prospect of seeing Mrs. Truman. She was astonished to see him but dreadfully upset. Not expecting him, she had made a previous engagement at the Shoreham Hotel and couldn't break it, for it had entailed rather elaborate preparations and involved several people and the food had already been ordered. The President of the United States had to eat alone and looked rather depressed at the prospect.

I actually recall that night rather clearly. I happened to see Mr. Truman as he sat at table for that solitary dinner. He reminded me of a lonely man rattling around in a big house when the wife's away. But Mrs. Truman knew her husband well and knew therefore how he'd feel, so she broke up her party as early as she could and got home to him. That was, and is, a most loving and close family, as I never tire of saying.

And now suddenly the 1952 Presidential campaign was upon us. And then, just as suddenly, it was past us and I had entered into an entirely new phase of my life. And I entered it with a bang—as the man responsible for keeping President-Elect Eisenhower safe and sound while he made good on his famous campaign promise, which, as I recall it, ran: "I shall go to Korea myself."

Somehow most people seem to think Mr. Eisenhower waited for several months before he redeemed that pledge to stop the Korean war personally. Nothing of the sort. He went there as President-elect only three weeks after he'd won the election from Adlai Stevenson.

The Secret Service, as you saw in the case of Mr. Kennedy, takes over full responsibility for the safety of the President-elect. When I learned that Mr. Eisenhower intended to go to Korea immediately, I dropped everything and gave my full attention to this project, examining it from every security angle possible.

The more I studied the situation, the less I liked the idea. It seemed incomparably dangerous to me. Roosevelt's trips to Casablanca, *et al.*, were extremely risky, of course, but they were outside an actual war zone. All of Korea was in flames, and, from all I could make out from intelligence reports, the savagery of our Chinese opponents made even the wartime Japanese seem relatively tame. I was certain they would do everything in their power to kill our President-elect, by bomb or booby trap, gun or poison—if they possibly could.

Actually one would have to go back to Lincoln to find any President-elect who had encountered a situation so full of hazard. Proslavery fanatics had threatened to kill Lincoln before he reached Washington to be inaugurated. He was warned and with good reason that his train, en route to his Inaugural, would be mobbed at Baltimore and that the mob would try to kill him. He was forced to travel incognito from Philadelphia to Washington because of the warning. Later he was

[155]

savagely attacked by Southern supporters for taking these precautions!

The Chief of the Secret Service, as I've noted, is empowered by law to forbid the President of the United States to undertake any venture or trip the Chief considers too dangerous. This veto power over the President has never been used on an important occasion but I seriously considered forbidding Mr. Eisenhower to go to Korea at that moment in history. In the end, however, I decided that the new President *must* do what he considered necessary for the public welfare no matter what the risk. With this decision made I plunged in, then, to the task of making this hair-raisingly dangerous trip as undangerous as I possibly could.

The newspapers and magazines called this trip "The Great Deception." This was because I had determined that our greatest defensive weapon must be secrecy and proceeded to organize one of the biggest hush-hush episodes in history. Talk about cloak-and-dagger atmospheres! Here are a few of the details which can now be revealed.

Before Mr. Eisenhower came to the White House he was head of Columbia University. Day and night his mansion at 60 Morningside Heights in New York City was surrounded by a swarm of reporters, office-seekers and the other impedimenta which encompass a President-elect's home. When we had set the exact moment of Mr. Eisenhower's departure, our chief secrecy problem was to smuggle him out of his house without arousing the curiosity of the press. The same secrecy had to surround the movements of all the other members of his party.

It may seem trifling from this distance in time, but a major problem, if we were to maintain our secrecy, was to get the President-elect's luggage out of his residence without the reporters noting it. We got some of it out by a simple device. We put several pieces of baggage in mail sacks and one of our agents, disguised as a mailman, lugged them out of the house. Down the street from the mansion, and with nobody watching, a Secret Service car picked this agent up and the "mail" was brought to the New York office of the Secret Service.

But there were still some important pieces of luggage left and I did not want to arouse suspicion by making the outgoing mail sack appear to be abnormally heavy. So we enlisted the aid of three maids at the residence.

One of the maids dressed herself in traveling clothes at our request. Laden with her bags she appeared at the front door of the President's house. The two other maids were with her to see her off on her "vacation." Now a Secret Service car pulled up in front of the door, ostensibly to take her and her luggage to Grand Central Station. Her friends waved good-by and she was off. The agent drove her two blocks to Broadway and dropped her there, then took the baggage on down to our headquarters. The maid had a cup of coffee, whiled away a little time, and then went back to work, via the rear entrance. Nobody caught on to the ruse.

Getting Mr. Eisenhower himself out of his home in as successfully casual a manner as we'd removed his luggage presented greater difficulty. It was necessary to schedule his departure for early in the morning—while it was still dark. The time and date finally agreed on was Saturday, November 29, 1952 at 5:45 A.M., an hour for the most secret of doings.

[157]

It was at that time that he would have to be at Mitchell Field, to leave by plane on the first leg of the long journey.

But before we decided on the precise plan for smuggling the President-elect out of his home that morning there was a prior problem we had to solve. We had to see to it that he wouldn't be missed by people as soon as he disappeared from view. Newspapermen, their sensibilities sharpened by day-and-night vigils before his house, seemed to pick up any unusual vibrations in the atmosphere. They would want to know where he was the moment he didn't show up in his normal spots.

Thus we had him remain within his residence for the few Saturdays which preceded his planned trip. Up until then he had been going to an office he maintained in the Commodore Hotel in midtown New York for Saturday appointments. Now our men subtly pointed out to newspapermen that Mr. Eisenhower was developing the habit of seeing people in his own home on Saturdays. The newspapermen registered the fact, apparently.

We also, with great ostentation, set up an elaborate series of appointments between Mr. Eisenhower and well-known members of his Cabinet—for the Saturday afternoon following his departure, and for Sunday and Monday as well.

For example, Secretary of State-designate John Foster Dulles appeared at the Morningside Heights residence to keep an appointment six hours after the President had taken off on his trip. This was as we had arranged and Mr.. Dulles spent some time alone in the inner sanctum where the President-elect usually held his private conferences. Then he emerged. To the assembled press he gave in minute detail a description of what he'd talked over with Mr. Eisenhower. He merely neglected to say that he'd talked these facts over with his chief a day or two before.

Other members of the President-elect's Cabinet did the same and in this way we were able to forestall any suspicions by members of the press who were not in on the conspiracy.

Actually getting Mr. Eisenhower himself out of his residence without attracting attention gave us considerable trouble. We first planned to sneak him out of the back entrance of his house, through a Columbia dormitory near by and then out the back entrance of this dormitory to a waiting car. Another idea was to have him dress up in a hat and coat belonging to one of the Secret Service agents who always accompanied him and who had the same general build as the President-elect. If a Secret Service agent entered a car at any hour of the day or night it could not possibly concern anybody.

Both plans were rejected. My reasoning was that, if either plan were uncovered *in medias res,* its very elaborateness would tip off the reporters that a story of major proportions was brewing. I decided to have Mr. Eisenhower embark from in front of his house in his usual manner.

A few minutes before the car he was to leave in pulled up quietly in front of the President-elect's mansion, the dome and sidelights in its interior were disconnected so that nobody could see who was inside when the door was opened. If those lights had been on they would have aroused the curiosity of any knowledgeable observer—for Attorney General-designate Brownell was in the car; he was to accompany Mr. Eisenhower to Korea.

[159]

The President-elect was ready and waiting and the moment the car arrived he slid out of his darkened house like a wraith, got into the darkened car without even saying hello and car and occupants moved slowly and quietly away from the curbing.

According to our plan, the automobile took the first right-hand turn off Morningside Heights. This turn was a signal for a car halfway down the block along which the Presidential car now moved to turn on its lights. The Presidential car sped past this waiting vehicle, which then was driven so that it lay right across the street and its motor was turned off. The driver of this car was, of course, a Secret Service agent. This stalled obstacle was just an extra precaution we took to block any wide-awake reporter who might have seen the President-elect leave and followed him. It served another purpose too; if a reporter had run after the Presidential car on foot for a block and then looked down the street it had turned into, the stalled car would have prevented him from seeing whether, in the next block, the Eisenhower car had turned north or south —that is, toward or away from the route to Mitchell Field. This might have prevented the reporter from making any positive decision about the probable destination of the President-elect.

Mr. Eisenhower was now driven to Mitchell Field. At the entrance to this airdrome his car doused its lights and followed an Air Force pilot car in total darkness to the waiting plane. Here Mr. Brownell and Mr. Eisenhower climbed out of their car and aboard the plane. At exactly 5:55 A.M. the historic journey was under way.

When I draw this picture of the Secret Service consciously

deceiving the great free press of the United States, I do not
want to give a false impression. This necessary security measure had been determined at a very high level of policy. And
the owners and managers of our major news-gathering media
were let in on the conspiracy of silence after the President
had left. But we dared not take the ordinary reporter in on
the secret even then. Actually, I even kept knowledge of the
trip from the agents who generally guarded Mr. Eisenhower,
excepting, naturally, those who were to go on the trip with
him.

You can't keep a President-elect missing for long, however, and so after the first three days of Mr. Eisenhower's absence the news leaked out to the men and women of the press.
However, not a single item was published (or, as far as I can
make out, even gossiped about in private) for six days, until
our President-elect had actually started on his homeward trip.
An hour after he'd left Korea all censorship was lifted on this
unprecedented news black-out. There followed a stream of
copy and a volume of broadcast words almost without parallel
in our history. However, nobody has published the view of
the Great Deception presented here until now.

I knew from Mr. Eisenhower's behavior in Korea that we
were going to have our hands full keeping him safe during
his administration. He was not only a man who was coura-
geous; he simply didn't know the meaning of fear. Communist snipers were everywhere in that benighted, forlorn and
freezing land. The front lines zigged and zagged and were
everywhere extremely fluid. Still he insisted on going up to
the very front of the front and my men guarding him had
their hearts in their mouths for his safety. On one occasion

he ate lunch in a spot where, the very next day, an American soldier was shot to death by a sniper. And several times he wandered into parts of the front which, an hour or two later, were captured by the enemy. Too, it was evident that he wasn't going to waste any time informing his guard about his movements. It was up to us, he seemed to imply, to keep up with him, even to be a jump ahead of him, for he often changed his plans in midstream.

I had gotten off on the wrong foot with the Eisenhowers at the start—and this was partly due to my new chief's penchant for taking off into the wild blue yonder without so much as a by-your-leave. Here's what happened.

On the night of the Presidential elections I had, as was my custom, two separate groups of agents standing by near to the candidates; one group of twelve men was at the Stevenson Headquarters in Chicago and one at the Eisenhower HQ in New York. Mr. Stevenson conceded early in the morning and at 4:50 A.M. the agent in charge of Mr. Eisenhower's guard called me at my home in Washington to inform me that the President-elect had decided to fly to his favorite golf club in Augusta, Georgia. He was going in the plane of a friend and, my man told me, there'd be room for only two Secret Service men on the plane. The President-elect, I was told, would be glad to see me the next day at his cottage on the golf links and discuss security plans for himself and his family.

I knew there'd be an awful crush of people in Augusta and I got on the phone to round up agents in Washington to get them down to Augusta quickly. However, I could only find two men—the rest were either en route back from the Stevenson unit or were occupied with Mr. Truman. I told the two

I had located to join President-Elect Eisenhower's party as soon as they could do so.

I knew four guards wouldn't be enough and I was right. The crowds were even greater than I had thought they'd be. President-Elect Eisenhower and his wife were separated from their son and grandchildren during an impromptu motorcade from the airfield to the golf course. They were, of course, very worried when this happened and though everybody finally got to the little cottage the Eisenhowers used at the Augusta Golf Club, an agent down there phoned me and told me that Mrs. Mamie Eisenhower had been somewhat critical of the Secret Service because of the misadventure. I could well understand her upset but the suddenness of the new President-elect's decision had left us without transportation or agents available. Even the Secret Service can't do the impossible if we aren't given time to plan.

Meanwhile I was going out of my mind trying to get transportation to Augusta myself. The planes from New York to Augusta were all jammed and I simply couldn't get passage on one. At last, however, my bad luck broke, and several other Secret Service agents and I were able to board a plane that got us in at 7:25 that night.

The agents who'd come with the President were on the point of collapse—they'd been on duty for forty-two hours steadily. I took over now and when, in a few hours, I'd been able to bring a little order into the surrounding chaos, I went over to see Mr. and Mrs. Eisenhower.

I explained to them what had happened as well as I could without sounding as though I were blaming Mr. Eisenhower's sudden departure to Augusta for the whole matter. However, they seemed to understand perfectly and were as gracious as they could be. I left feeling a little relieved but also realizing that I'd have to be on the *qui vive* with this great man, and that I was going to face problems quite different from those I'd been up against before. Just how different I was soon to learn.

The interregnum, the period between the election of a new President and his inauguration, is a sad and rather difficult time for those of us who must stay on after the departure of the outgoing regime. Attachments and loyalties made over the years must be suddenly broken and leavetakings made. At the same time one must brisk up one's spirit for the encounter with the new regime, with its fresh and unfamiliar personalities and its unique problems.

Up till the last day I was pretty much able to bury my conflicting feelings in work—chiefly, now, preparations for the inauguration of Mr. Eisenhower. I have described such preparations in the section on Truman's inauguration and since one inauguration is basically similar to another I will not again go into the elaborate security precautions we take. A few details, however, may be interesting.

A part of the huge Inaugural Parade which precedes the swearing-in ceremony is made up of floats. I had to check every detail of these floats to see that there were no weapons or explosives concealed on them. Assassination plots of this kind using innocent-looking vehicles have been directed against leaders of states successfully and I was not going to let any assassins use this obvious method of getting close to my charges, for the floats had to pass the Presidential reviewing stand in front of the White House.

The Kennedy Inauguration when the lectern caught fire, one of the many worrying experiences in the life of Secret Service Chief U. E. Baughman, who is indicated with an arrow. (James McNamara, Washington *Post*)

Secret Service men surround the Presidential car. President Truman can be seen through the windshield in the back seat.

U. E. Baughman shows President Eisenhower reproductions of counterfeit money. (Associated Press photo)

Protecting the President involves many changes of scene and costume. Here is U. E. Baughman on an Eisenhower fishing trip, and attending a formal affair with Mrs. Baughman.

President Harry S. Truman sets out on his well-known early-morning constitutional. He gave the Secret Service quite a shock the first time he did this.

The kind of situation Secret Service men hate. Eisenhower in Korea is surrounded by an enthusiastic crowd. The car can't move forward —perfect for an assassin. (Republic of Korea, Office of Public Information)

Scene in front of Blair House shortly after two Puerto Rican nationalists attempted to assassinate President Truman. (Harris and Ewing)

Donald T. Birdzell, White House police officer, was fired on by Collazo and hit in both knees. (Harris and Ewing)

Torresola, one of the assassins, was shot down and killed on the Blair House lawn. (Harris and Ewing)

Angry mobs threatened Nixon in Lima during his South American tour (above) but it was in Caracas that mob violence became mortally dangerous. Secret Service decision to use a closed car undoubtedly saved the lives of Vice President and Mrs. Nixon. Shown below is Nixon's car, the windows smashed by stones and clubs.

For the Secret Service any crowd or public event is a source of worry and potential danger. Constant vigilance must be maintained. Here U. E. Baughman attends two contrasting functions: above with President Eisenhower at the Tomb of the Unknown Soldier at the Arc de Triomphe in Paris, and below with President Kennedy at a ball game in Washington. (Cecil W. Stoughton, White House Army Signal Agency)

The New Hampshire float caused me some small concern. It called for a girl to stand on the rear right side (the reviewing stand side) with a .12-gauge shotgun in her hand. I've forgotten now what the New Hampshire tableau was supposed to portray, probably the settlement of New England. I weighed the matter mightily for some time but in the end I yielded to the near-tearful importuning of the New Hampshire float-makers and reluctantly gave my permission for the young lady to carry her gun. I stipulated, however, that the shotgun and the pretty New Hampshire miss must both be thoroughly checked out by one of my agents *after* she'd mounted the float on the day of the parade. Even so I didn't like it.

The Secret Service also had a rule that nothing must be thrown toward the President if we can possibly prevent it. Thus I had to veto the plan of those in charge of the Texas float to throw roses toward the Presidential stand. I pointed out that it would be just as effective to throw them forward of their cart as they approached and rearward as they left the Presidential stand behind.

One thing always happens before inaugurations. The Chief of the Secret Service is hounded by the big automobile manufacturers, trying to sell him on the idea of letting their particular brand of car lead the Inaugural Parade. In vain I've always told them that not I but the Inaugural Committee decides on this matter. I suppose they reasoned that if I decided that the President's security counseled the use of their car as against another I could swing the committee my way. Hour after hour these calls came in, interrupting important work, and while I yield to no man in my admiration of enterprise, I will now grant that there can be too much of this good thing. Finally I besought the Inauguration Committee to come to a decision. They did, choosing Cadillacs to lead the way. And my phone calls subsided abruptly.

On January 15, five days before the Inauguration, I went to New York to confer with Secret Service agents there about a particularly complicated and dangerous forgery case, and also to inspect the plans I had put in effect for Mr. Eisenhower's security. While checking dispositions of my agents in the corridor outside of his office in the Commodore Hotel I ran into the President-elect himself. He was more than cordial and invited me to have lunch with him and his very dear friend Aksel Nielsen, whom he'd known since he'd been a major in the army and with whom he still went hunting and fishing.

In view of Mr. Eisenhower's later illness, which some people have suggested may have resulted from a trencherman's disposition, I can say that the menu for this meal would indicate quite the opposite. There was no cocktail beforehand. We had a tomato juice and this was followed by an aspic salad; for dessert we had fresh fruit and coffee.

It was at this luncheon that I realized that a major part of my security plans for the new President would center around golf.

First Mr. Eisenhower asked me if I had any objections to his plans for playing golf at the Burning Tree Club, a course in suburban Maryland not too far from the White House. I gave him a tentative "No, I didn't see any objections," but I told him I'd check the course forthwith and let him have my final thoughts on the matter.

At one point the talk lapsed for a moment and Mr. Eisenhower seemed to be staring dreamily into space. Then he suddenly asked me: "What's the distance from the South Portico of the White House to the fence that surrounds the grounds?"

I calculated rapidly. "About two hundred yards," I said.

"Great," he said. "It'll be just perfect for a nine iron. And maybe I can get a little sand in there and if I can I'll be able to practice my wedge shots too."

"Certainly you could," I said.

As soon as I got back to Washington I called the White House Police and had them measure the exact distance from the South Portico to the fence. I hadn't been far off. It was 750 feet or 250 yards.

At this point I launched a few informal inquiries about the possibility of getting some kind of imitation sand bunker on the White House lawn—just to be informed in case the subject came up. I studied the rear of the White House from the security standpoint. And I also sent some agents over to make a thorough check on the Burning Tree Club. I asked my men to give me detailed security recommendations after their check.

On January 19, the day before the Inauguration, I paused in my activities and girded up my emotional nature for a spell of deep feeling. It was the day for leavetakings. These could not be postponed any longer, for the next day would be too laden with activities to say good-by properly. I went to the office of my chief first, Secretary of the Treasury Snyder. And I also paid my respects to Ed Foley, Under Secretary of the Treasury, and my immediate superior. They were both cordial and highly complimentary in their remarks to me and I was sorry to terminate my relationship with them. Then I went in search of President Truman.

I caught up with him as he was taking a dip in the White House swimming pool. This was where I had first met him. He got out of the pool and gave me a watery handshake and although I am usually fairly articulate in most situations I suddenly found myself at a loss for words. And I could feel myself uncomfortably close to certain emotions that Chiefs don't generally admit to having. The President, as always, divined what the other person was going through and tried to put me at my ease and to that end he chatted about this and that. Finally I summoned up the ability to say good-by without breaking down and I did so. Of the entire conversation, which must have lasted some ten minutes, I can only recall one sentence of what this fine man said. It was a characteristic salty Trumanism. "I don't know what I may have accomplished," he told me, "but I sure have made a lot of people squirm."

Of the Inauguration itself I recall two incidents, one funny, homely thing and one sad and upsetting.

The first: The President-elect at the very last moment couldn't find his white dress tie and there were no haberdashery stores open. Somehow his baggage had gotten lost en route from New York and he was stranded without a tie for his Inauguration. The agent who called me to report on this security problem was vastly upset (he hadn't been anywhere near so upset after the Blair House shooting, in which he'd participated) and I calmed him down by taking a firm, authoritative line. "Give the President-elect," I said firmly, "your own tie and cover *your* neck with your silk scarf until I get another one over to you." I quickly called my wife and she got one of mine over to my office by taxi. It was all a tempest in a teapot, however, for just as the cab arrived with my tie I got an "all-clear" from my man at the White House. The President-elect's baggage had been located, he informed me, and the emergency was over. I put the tie I'd gotten in a little-used filing cabinet and it turned up five years later, good as new in shape but an interesting meerschaum hue from the intervening years.

The second incident, the saddening one, was the coolness which developed between Mr. Truman and Mr. Eisenhower, perhaps over some issues that had been raised in the heat of the campaign.

Mr. Truman, reporting on the whole affair, has said that he and his wife had planned, as was the custom, to have the President-elect over for an informal White House luncheon just before the Inauguration ceremonies were to begin.

"We were disappointed when the invitation was refused," Mr. Truman said. "General Eisenhower chose to arrive at the White House when there was only enough time to go to the Capitol for the taking of the Presidential oath." Mr. Truman canceled the lunch and then proceeded to wait for Mr. Eisenhower to present himself at the White House.

They did drive together to the Capitol but continued to be distinctly cool to each other—and are to this day.

We who stayed on to serve under Mr. Eisenhower were the losers because of this high-level fracas. Mr. Truman never again, to my knowledge, visited the White House during the Eisenhower Administration. Nor was he consulted nor called upon to serve. And this was altogether too bad from the standpoint of those who had been close to him for so long.

And thus ended the reign of Harry Truman—characteristically not with a whimper but with a bang. It had been more than merely a privilege to protect his life and the lives of all the members of his family.

Mr. Truman did not return to the White House that afternoon after the swearing-in ceremony, nor did Mrs. Truman nor Margaret. Instead they went directly to Union Station and, with very little fanfare and no Secret Service guard, they embarked for their home in Missouri, leaving the pomp and the ceremony of the White House and the Presidency behind them forever.

A Brand-New White House

HOW DOES THE SECRET SERVICE PROTECT THE President and his family when they are at the White House? I have purposely postponed discussing this problem while telling about the Truman era because till almost the very end of his administration Mr. Truman lived at Blair House across Pennsylvania Avenue from the White House. The Trumans had been forced to move out of the White House in 1948 because the whole place had become a firetrap and a hazard to safety. And they did not move back till March of 1952, less than a year before they were to leave the Presidential residence for good.

Thus the story of the elaborate security measures which were set up, gradually, for the new White House concerns the Eisenhowers for the most part. And these measures I will relate in terms of the new incumbents, though of course the same general protective measures were also carried out for the Trumans.

The Presidential home the Eisenhowers came into was a far cry from the White House of yesteryear. That edifice had been reconstructed in 1818, after having been gutted by fire when the British burned Washington in the War of 1812. The South Portico was added in 1824 and the huge North Portico five years later.

After that for 120 years President after President had carved the place up as he saw fit. As each modern convenience came along it was put into the old wood frame. As one account had it: "Pipes and wires honeycombed the walls for running water, gas, central heating and electricity. Each convenience and structural change took its toll in weakened walls, sagging floors and precarious ceilings."

When Margaret Truman's piano went through the floor of her sitting room and, at a gala reception, the great chandelier in the Blue Room swayed and tinkled dangerously in an edificial paroxysm it was abundantly clear that a checkup had to be made. The checkup was made and one of the investigators put the case against the old White House succinctly: "It was," he said, "standing up purely from habit."

The venerable ark that housed our former Presidents was once described by President Fillmore as "a temple of inconvenience." And Andrew Jackson had said of one section: "Hell itself couldn't warm that corner."

The new building, however, is a marvel. The old innards were taken completely out and the builders started from scratch. The new building is now supported by a steel skeleton embedded in a very deep foundation and is virtually indestructible.

It is a marvel of comfort and luxury. Tremendous machines in the basement and subbasement now keep it warm or cool in the proper seasons with great and simple efficiency. It is up to date from kitchen to solarium and its occupants can complain no more of the slightest inconvenience in this great building.

The White House has 132 rooms in it. The forty men I kept on active duty in the White House Detail of the Secret Service would not be nearly enough to insure the safety of the President and his family while they inhabit this huge building. And so we come to the White House Police Force, a small army of hand-picked men which the Chief of the Secret Service directs and supervises.

This corps is the President's "standing guard," so to speak (as distinguished from the mobile White House Detail, which moves with the President wherever he goes, including back to the White House when he goes there), and it is considered one of the finest police forces in the world. I generally secured these men from Washington, D.C.'s Metropolitan Police Force, one of the crack units in the country.

Before a new man is taken on the White House Police Force he is put through a series of physical and mental tests that would root out anybody who wasn't perfectly balanced men-

SECRET SERVICE CHIEF

tally and very healthy physically. Every one of these men is an expert marksman and is familiar with every kind of firearm. They have one of the finest (if not the finest) police pistol teams of all time and usually walk away with the top awards when they compete with other high-ranking police bodies throughout the world.

These keen, alert men are stationed strategically throughout the White House according to a master plan I worked out. The basis of the plan is our old friend "protection in depth," which I've discussed before. The White House Police are arranged in concentric circles around the First Family's permanent establishment. The inner circle completely surrounds the Presidential living quarters within the White House. The outer perimeter of this uniformed guard is at the White House gates, which are placed at intervals in the fence that surrounds the White House grounds. In general these men are arranged according to the following principle: the closer to the living quarters of the family they are, the greater is their numerical concentration; the farther off, the lesser.

Every doorway through which an intruder might pass in the White House (no matter how obscure or apt to be "forgotten" the section of the house may be where the door is) is fully guarded. Since there are many, many passageways and doorways you can see why we must have a minimum of thirty-six policemen on duty all the time.

In addition to the White House Police, which is under the command of Major Ralph Stover, the nonuniformed elite guard is still the White House Detail. When Mr. Eisenhower came into the White House, I retained Jim Rowley to head this group. He had been with the White House Detail since

FDR's time and is an experienced man in this kind of work. He or his immediate assistant is always with the President when he leaves the White House. Rowley tries to visualize in advance all the eventualities that might befall his charge and thinks up ways to circumvent, forestall or prevent them entirely.

The White House Detail forms its own separate concentric circles around the First Family in residence. Again the greatest concentration of manpower is at the center and this thins out toward the periphery. I have stationed these men in strategic spots selected so that if a crisis should occur they can take over the tactical deployment of the White House Police.

Obviously, with such a guard, the mentally disturbed would have small opportunity to get close to the President in his White House quarters. What, then, do we consider the other dangers we must protect him against?

To answer that, let us look at the people who service the White House. There are about four thousand of them, ranging from laundrymen to leaf-rakers, from telephone operators to air-conditioning experts, from scullery maids to chambermaids to chefs. We feel it is absolutely necessary to keep an eye on each and every one of them. Therefore each of them must have a security check made on him, to establish that he is not subversive of course, but mainly that he is not insane or potentially insane.

Have these intensive checkups proved their worth? Again are we being "too careful"?

To my mind just one case in point would justify all this elaborate precaution. And I could tell two dozen. The following one concerns a man who had applied for the job of servicing the White House air conditioners. A first check on him showed nothing, but our second routine check showed he had been a leading member of the Communist Party in the District of Columbia for twenty years. The very idea of a Communist being that close to the major ventilators in the White House even for a moment is enough to give a man like myself a very heavy shudder!

All people who get our official okay are given a pass made up in a special division of the Secret Service. The pass has been designed by printing experts and the chances of a potential assassin making a successful counterfeit of one barely exists. Two thousand of these passes are held by service and tradespeople who must enter the White House daily.

About two thousand more people who come to the White House do not have to appear sufficiently often to require a permanent pass. These people are checked on less thoroughly and are given badges, also designed and printed under our supervision. When these individuals present themselves at the White House gate they are given a special guard who stays with them until they leave.

How might a potential assassin strike within the White House?

Certainly by attempting to poison the food. Members of the White House staff have been so thoroughly checked that they are totally above suspicion or reproach. So a poisoner would have to reach the food before it arrived at the White House.

When food is purchased for the President's table it must be bought only at stores that have been officially checked and okayed by the Secret Service. The entire personnel of these

stores have received a security check and every new em-
ployee must be scrutinized thoroughly.

To make assurance doubly sure, however, a White House
Police officer accompanies the White House staff members
whenever a purchase of food is made. This food is immediately put into a receptacle brought by the officer, who then
locks it with a special key and accompanies the food back to
the White House. He now keeps it under surveillance until
it is locked into the White House larder.

Science has put new and terrible weapons into the hands
of potential assassins. We must be, and are, constantly on the
alert in the White House against atomic debris, bacteria and
gases.

Our apprehension about these weapons is not at all far-
fetched. The Russians already have used atomic dust against
a defector from their cause who fled from East to West Germany in an attempt to escape their wrath, according to one
report. He did not escape, even though they dared not openly
kidnap him. Instead they put atomic dust in this man's coffee.
The unfortunate man slowly lost his teeth, his hearing, his
hair, his sight and then patches of his skin began to come off
as the terrible poison did its work. It is only fair to say that
this story could be pure rumor—though I myself tend to believe it.

The White House is checked very carefully for any indications of atomic dust. Regularly I sent agents through all the
rooms with Geiger counters. And I made a daily spot check
with a new, simplified radiation-detection device. This con-
sists of a film which can detect radioactivity. An agent carries
a piece of this film into key rooms in the White House and

then has the film "developed"—that is, put through a test which will determine whether it has passed through any radioactivity.

At this writing plans for protection against the very real threat from atomic debris call for the construction of a special alarm system in the White House. This would set off a warning bell if anybody should, with or without malice aforethought, come into the President's residence with any of that unhappy dust on his person.

In a democracy we cannot, as dictatorships can, ring our leaders round with a solid wall of steel and human flesh. To my way of thinking, the protection the Secret Service gives the President of the United States in his official residence is the greatest that can be given to a man under our political system.

chapter   14

Golf, Gettysburg and Grandchildren

FROM THE SECURITY STANDPOINT I DIVIDE THE
kinds of problems presented by the Eisenhower Administration into three distinct parts—problems that preceded the heart
attack and the ileitis, the problems that occurred during those
illnesses, and the problems that followed on them. From my
view Mr. Eisenhower was a very different man after his illnesses and this change made it necessary to develop new security approaches.

Before his heart attack the chief problems we had to encounter were those which, in my office, were semijocularly referred to as the Three G's—Golf, Gettysburg and Grand-children. Of course the Three G's stayed with us during the entire eight years he was in office. But, after a bit, we'd worked out solutions to the major problems they posed.

In his book *Gamesmanship* Stephen Potter calls golf "the game's game of games' games" and by these magnificently absurd six words of nonsense he makes it ultimately clear that of all the sports man has developed with which to test himself physically and mentally golf is the testingest game of all. Anybody who has ever teed off in front of a small gathering of friends knows how that tiny white ball can grow smaller and smaller as you address it before the public gaze, and how the slightest distraction, a caddy moving, a slight cough from the gallery, can reduce one to a kind of condensed idiocy complicated by total blindness.

Imagine, then, the test it would be for a man who must play the game surrounded by eight to twelve other men carrying long-range rifles and machine guns, and stealthily poking around him, before and aft. I think the fact that Dwight D. Eisenhower persevered in his love for the game of golf under these conditions (for these were the ones I visited upon him) is proof enough of the toughness of the spirit that made him great. As one golf professional said of him after witnessing the process for eighteen holes: "If I knew nothing more about him than that he still wants to play with all those men around him and still plays a very good game, I'd know enough to vote for him."

This of course is a light approach to this subject. But when Jim Rowley and I came to examine the problems raised by

Mr. Eisenhower's dedication to golf we realized that they were deadly serious. And we had to face up to these problems almost at once for Mr. Eisenhower did not let any grass grow under his golfing shoes. The first day he went to Burning Tree as President was on February 14, less than a month after the Inauguration.

A golf course is almost a perfect place for an assassination attempt. If the killer is an expert marksman the high ground at most courses gives him an excellent shot at objects below. Also, the trees and shrubs that bound fairways afford perfect concealment. Then on a golf course one knows the exact route the potential victim will take. And the fact that one's putative target plays a course regularly or even fairly regularly gives plenty of opportunity to work out the details of the plan; I mean, one need not rush into one's assassination attempt.

These considerations chilled my blood as I discussed them with Jim Rowley. "All a man really needs if he's serious," Jim told me, "is a high-powered rifle with a telescopic sight. And he also stands a good chance of getting away from his pursuers after the kill from that distance."

I was to remember Jim's words years later, when assassins tried to kill Alberto Lleras Camargo, the former President of Colombia, on a golf course. They fired four shots at him from a rifle at a great distance while he was playing on a remote section of the links. There was a suspicion that the attempt on Camargo's life was fomented by the Communists but the charge couldn't be proved, for at such a distance it's possible to kill a man, or at least try to, and still make good an escape, and these men did just that.

With such thoughts in mind Jim and I laid down the plans
that ever afterward were observed in protecting Mr. Eisenhower on the golf links. Wherever the President played, there
were always men who went in advance to flush out any potential marksman. This advance party always numbered from one
to three men dressed in golf clothes and carrying golf bags.
They went toward the highest point of ground and surveyed
the surroundings from that vantage point.

Two more agents dressed in golf clothes and carrying golf
bags flanked Mr. Eisenhower to his left and to his right. In
their bags, instead of golf clubs, they carried high-powered
(.351) rifles with the highest-powered telescopic sights available. The same kind of rifle was also carried by the advance
scouts and thus we could be certain that our firepower would
carry to any distance that a sharpshooter might snipe from.

Two other agents followed behind the President. One traveled on foot and one in a powered golf cart. The latter carried
a machine gun concealed in the cart. Jim Rowley and I decided
that this gun was a necessity on the course; for it would have
been possible for a group of would-be assassins to rush the
Presidential party. In such a case a machine gun is always the
weapon of choice, for it can handle several assassin types at
the same time.

All of the protective agents on the golf course were tied
together by a walkie-talkie system. The central control station
for this was in the clubhouse and it was permanently manned
whenever the President was on the golf course. The agent in
the golf cart would report to this control station at every new
tee and every green so that in case of an emergency reinforcements or medical aid or whatever was needed could be sent to

the President's exact location. This was all logged into a permanent record.

People who knew about the advance scouts always asked me whether they ever came across anything suspicious.

Not really. They came across several spooners, a flock of neckers and some petters, but investigation always showed that these couples were out there in the rough for relatively legitimate reasons. A few poachers were turned up but they too were not assassination types, just good honest clean-cut American poachers. Once an advance agent came across two small lads lying on their stomachs under a bush with a loaded .22 rifle between them. It gave our man a bad turn, what with delinquency being what it is today. But the boys weren't Presidential thrill killers, just nine-year-old Huck Finns from the area who were out squirrel hunting and got a sudden hankering to see the President of the United States.

We enlisted the help of local and state police to patrol the roads (some of them small, isolated country lanes) around any course when the President was there. For some time the Augusta National Golf Club did not have a hurricane fence around it and this worried me some, for it seemed to be an open invitation to prowlers and the curious if not the insane. At length, however, a quiet campaign by Cliff Roberts, Chairman of the Augusta Club, to have a fence put up around the course finally paid off. I breathed more easily after it was erected.

Indeed, the new President had only been in office one month when Cliff Roberts told me that they were going to build President Eisenhower his own special house overlooking the famous eighteenth hole. And build the house they did in a very few months. It became known at once by two titles—Mamie's Cabin and the Little White House. Actually the latter title fitted it best, for just as President Truman treasured his stays at his white frame house in Key West so Mr. Eisenhower loved to spend his free time and his vacations with his cronies at the Augusta Club.

I myself was relieved when this house was built, for Mr. and Mrs. Eisenhower had up till then been quartered while there in cabins used by other people. This always meant that we had to go in and make a thorough inspection of the cabin before the Eisenhowers moved in—a larger undertaking than it sounds, as I will later indicate.

The new "cabin" turned out to be a plush, two-story, six-room cottage, beautifully decorated and with every modern convenience. One close observer of the President called it "Ike's Pleasure" for much of it had his favorite pastimes in mind. A handsome up-to-the-minute kitchen completely stocked would allow him to indulge his hobby of whipping up culinary treats for his friends on the spur of the moment. A studio room with every kind of oil paint and stacks of canvases allowed him to indulge his painting hobby whenever he was so minded. And all the facilities for his favorite indoor game, bridge, were there, including a plethora of partners in the clubhouse proper. The club even had its artificial lake specially stocked with fish so that the President could engage in his second-favorite outdoor sport without leaving the grounds.

The new cabin presented no protection problems for the Secret Service, situated as it was in open ground, surrounded by friendly people. We kept our concentric rings of men around the President and that was pretty much all that was needed.

Another new home the Eisenhowers soon purchased and reconstructed, however, required some of our very best and most concentrated planning along security lines. I refer to the first real home of their own the President and his lady had ever had in their (till then) thirty-eight years of marriage, the farm they now bought at Gettysburg, Pennsylvania.

This is really a very large place and, I knew at once, would take a *lot* of protecting. It is a century-old farmhouse, located on 189 acres of softly sloping meadow. The farmhouse is thought to have been used as a hospital for Confederate soldiers during the famous Battle of Gettysburg.

In all directions except south the borders of the President's land were five hundred yards from his house, a good respectable distance in a security officer's book. And I was relieved to find that the land to the south, which lay only one hundred yards away, had just recently been bought by General Arthur Nevins, who had served with General Eisenhower in Europe and was then one of his closest friends. That meant we had plenty of space on all sides in which to set up defenses.

First we decided to have a special guardhouse erected close to the farm and in a commanding position on the driveway which led to the residence from the main road. The driveway was a long one and so, although a guard was always stationed at the gate, we had a "road alarm" installed for double measure. This was made up of pneumatic tubes set right into the ground. Any person or vehicle coming up the road would pass over these tubes and the pressure would set off a warning signal in the guardhouse.

Surrounding the "yard" area (that is, the sections of the lawn people would be apt to stroll in or play games in) an electric-eye fence was erected. The esthetic advantage of this was that guests would not know of its existence and the practical one was that if any unwanted prowlers came around it would set off an alarm in the guardhouse when their bodies broke the circuit.

Of all the devices used, our nighttime "black lights" were the most up-to-the-minute scientifically. (Don't forget, this was some time back now.) These were infrared lights which could be turned on after dark. Nobody would know they were on unless they had, as we did, special binoculars. With these binoculars we could literally see in the dark, and unless a prowler also had such special glasses he would not know he was under our surveillance.

The trickiest gadget we rigged up was invented by Robert Bouck. You've met him before as head of our Protective Research section. He is one of the cleverest men I have ever known on the scientific side of police work, a true genius. The gadget he worked out now was a window screen for use in the roooms of the Eisenhower grandchildren when they came to visit.

The problem was to get a screen which would set off an alarm in the guardhouse if a kidnaper should break through our outer perimeter of defense and actually get to the children's bedroom windows. It was a grisly thought but our job was to foresee such unpleasant eventualities and guard against them.

With an ordinary all-metal screen the kind of alarm system

we needed was impossible. The metal would interfere with the electronic signal. Mr. Bouck thus purchased screens made of ordinary plastic mesh—then new on the market. He pulled out every twenty-fifth strand of this mesh and wove tiny metal wires in place of the plastic strand. These wires were then attached to an electric signal in the guardhouse. The screens were installed in the windows so firmly that they could not possibly be removed by force—a kidnaper thus would have to cut through them. This would have broken the signal in the guardhouse and tripped the alarm, bringing agents swarming to the scene.

In the end I was fairly satisfied with the security arrangements at Gettysburg—except for one thing. For several years I worried about a tourist observation tower at the top of Cemetery Ridge on the Gettsyburg Battlefield which overlooked the Eisenhower demesne. I knew that a good marksman with a high-powered rifle outfitted telescopically could shoot anyone wandering around on the Eisenhower farm from that tower. I had proposed keeping the tower closed and guarded when the family was at the farm. But Mr. Eisenhower had considered this too fussy and I was unable to get approval for my wish.

For several years the President tended to take security measures a little too lightly for my personal taste. But by a kind of wordless proselytizing I had gradually gotten him to change his mind slightly. His conversion became complete, however, when he finally read a book called *The Assassins,* a terrifying account of seven attempts that have been made on the lives of our Presidents throughout history—three, as you know, successful. After Mr. Eisenhower had read that book he agreed readily that the tower be shut when the family was in residence.

Speaking of Supervising Agent Bouck's ingenuity with the window screen brings up the third security problem that was new for us—the protection of the President's grandchildren. There were four of them (ultimately) and they were all lovely children. Their names, going from oldest to youngest, are David, Barbara Ann, Susan and Mary Jane. Taking care of them presented some very merry and lighthearted moments— and, for the agents on duty, some very difficult ones too.

Colonel (at that time Major) John, the children's father, was in the armed services, of course, and for a while moved about from place to place. However, the protective work we did for his family while he was stationed at Alexandria, Virginia, was typical of all the rest and I will describe that here. If I can give an adequate picture of that, you will grasp what the protection of children in a Presidential family involves.

Basically this is the story of the Station Wagon Command Post of the United States Secret Service—a very famous and much loved post for a while in Alexandria. And here is how it came to be founded and to function.

When Colonel John Eisenhower was sent to Alexandria he was able, despite the housing shortage, to locate and rent a very modest home in a middle-class neighborhood of that city. This home had a small front yard and was situated on a dead-end street.

Now it takes a minimum of three Secret Service agents to adequately protect each child in the Presidential menage; this puts each man on eight-hour duty, the most I like any agent to work, for more than that cuts down on his alertness.

Whenever a group of agents must protect people over an expanse of territory, it is necessary to set up a central post to co-ordinate activities. And, in the case of the house at Alexandria, the agents also had to have a place to sit when they got a little time off from their duties, a half-hour or hour or so—and there was no place to sit around Colonel Eisenhower's home and in that neighborhood there was nothing but other private houses.

The headquarters these twelve men set up therefore was a black nine-seater Pontiac station wagon, which they semipermanently immured in the driveway of Major Eisenhower's house. This nine-seater was a marvel of compactness.

The men ran specially insulated lines from the public utilities right into this command post on wheels—and the utilities companies tacked their meters on the side of the car. We had a telephone in there that was hooked up to the regular system, and another one that was connected directly with the White House. An electric outlet for a heater was also installed to keep the men warm; the temperatures at Alexandria often dipped to ten degrees or lower.

Also, the men had rigged up an "electric-eye" fence, the same type as at Gettysburg, and this completely surrounded the house itself. If tipped, this system would set off an alarm in the Pontiac. Then a thermal-type fire alarm was put up in the house and the bell for this was also installed in the nine-seater. There was in addition a direct telephone to the Alexandria Police Department for use in an emergency. And the car was also equipped with a portable two-way radio to be used as the check-in point for the other agents when they were out with their particular charge or charges.

But even this was not all the equipment in Fort Pontiac. The car also contained a riot gun and a machine gun in case of attack by several people at once. There were also eighteen gas masks for the agents and the entire Eisenhower family and, in preparation for any emergency that could possibly be imagined, food rations for crew and Eisenhowers which would last a week.

In short, the station wagon fort combined, in a miniature and overcrowded way, many of the protective functions of the main headquarters of the Secret Service in Washington. From this post even mail and packages were carefully screened and the potentially dangerous separated from the innocent. And all visitors were checked out.

Day after day, month after month, through rain, sleet and sunshine, the Station Wagon Command Post stood in the Eisenhower driveway. It slowly became an institution in the area. The men I'd selected had been carefully hand-sorted, had to have, in addition to their fine qualities as agents, a genuine and known love of children. This was not always an easy attribute to spot but I must have had some luck in my choices for David and Barbara Ann, Susan and Mary Jane came to adore their protectors.

The young ones of course became very fond of individual agents. We had to be careful that this relationship did not become too intense, for, sooner or later, the agent and the child must be separated and the parents wanted to be certain that the separation was not emotionally difficult. Thus I had to change the personnel guarding the children every so often.

It became a very nice matter to decide just exactly when the children were getting a bit too attached to the men—and vice versa, for it was often enough quite a wrench for these men, who had a particular fondness for youngsters.

I cannot leave this account without telling of the experiences of two of our agents who had to guard young Barbara Ann when she went to an all-girls camp one summer when she was twelve. When it became certain she was going I had to pick and choose with great discrimination for the project gave promise of requiring the greatest tact and the utmost delicacy—the kind a bull might need in a china shop if he were intent on establishing good relations rather than letting things deteriorate the way, we are taught, they so often do with bulls in china shops.

I selected two very intelligent and steady-on chaps, both married, both in their early thirties. Their names, so that posterity may know, were Max Phillips and Bert de Freese.

As far as I know, these two men were the first Secret Service agents ever to be assigned to guard duty at a girls' camp. The name of the place was Camp Allegheny and it was located in West Virginia. The children lived in tents while there and the agents too were quartered in one, just thirty yards down the camp street from Barbara Ann in an area called the Junior Tent section. Barbara Ann at the time had achieved, in camp parlance, the dizzy rank of Tentling, though I have never been entirely clear just what rights and privileges the clearly exalted title carried with it.

The grown-up camp staff later confessed it had held its collective breath when the agents first arrived. However, the two male Campfire Girl recruits were the souls of discretion.

They were there to see that the little girl remained safe and they did not interfere with her fun.

The very opposite of what was expected happened, however. Barbara Ann's Tentling compatriots, far from finding the two agents inhibiting, were simply *delighted* with them and completely accepted them into the very heart of camp life. The two were made Honorary Members of Indian Tribes sacred to Camp Allegheny. They were asked to dance around ritual fires, participate in solemn pledges of eternal friendship, to listen to the secrets of the Tentling code, and become, generally, part and parcel of camp life.

Perhaps what is most strange is that the two grown men, one thirty-five and the other thirty, loved the whole thing, the overnight camping trips, the sing-outs, the stories around the campfires before bedtime—all of it. "It was one of the finest times I have ever had," Mr. Phillips freely admits, "and highly instructive too. I learned more about woodlore, I think, than the girls themselves."

The statement is a kind of whimsical proof that the ideal I held out for my agents was indeed practicable. "You should be able," I told them, "to go anywhere, mix with any kind of group and quickly be accepted as one of them."

chapter **15**

Birds of Various Colors

As I HAVE SAID EARLIER, THE SECRET SERVICE IS
responsible for protecting our currency from all dangers to it.
I have already described counterfeiting at some length. But it
is only *one* of the manifold attacks criminals can make on our
money; they have a host of other nefarious activities which
keep our fifty-nine branches on permanent overtime, to leave
quite unmentioned what they do to the Chief's time. These
crimes include, among others, illegal trading in gold, the theft
and forgery of government bonds, the stealing of money from
our two Mints, and the forgery of government-issued checks.

Stories and lore have accumulated around each of these

crimes. Here are a few facts and a few tales selected almost at random from my bulging files.

I'll start with the most important of these law-breaking activities, the stealing and forging of government checks.

This is a streamlined, up-to-date crime par excellence, the product of a modern government's concern for the economic security of its citizens. Well over 400,000,000 government checks are issued every year; Social Security checks, veteran disability checks, unemployment checks, armed services checks —and all go through the United States mails.

These checks have been from the beginning a lodestone for the petty thief. Rifling mailboxes, though a Federal offense, became a favorite pastime for the underworld some twenty-five years ago. To show the growth in check-stealing and check-forging: in 1936 the Secret Service handled 5,000 such cases—by 1944 this had grown to 15,000 cases; today we handle over 40,000 annually and have developed a permanent backlog of over 22,000 cases—at least it's permanent until Congress gives us enough money to get abreast of the problem.

The crime of check-stealing was attractive to thieves for two reasons—the ease with which mailboxes could be opened and the ease with which merchants could be hoodwinked into cashing these stolen checks.

The fact is that the toughest mailbox locks are "easy pickings" for a thief. He can break into one in seconds, using a celluloid mandolin pick, or any other stiff, pliant material, to push back the catch of the lock. His main problem is to get to the box before the box owner does.

Mailbox owners waiting for government checks are notoriously prompt about getting to their mail. To solve this problem one thief we picked up had a motor scooter so that he could cover as many buildings as possible each morning before the box owners got to their boxes. Another bought a souped-up jalopy from a teen-ager for the same purpose. The fastest thief I ever encountered in this racket was arrested right here in Washington, D.C. He removed the entire back of a mailbox and each morning he would conceal himself in a recess behind it. From this vantage point he could pluck the checks out of the slots as fast as the postman dropped them in.

But check-stealing would never have grown to such dimensions were it not for the gullibility of shopkeepers. Some thieves were able to do a thriving business with no more identification than a forged Social Security card and/or a fishing license with the name of the payee of the check forged on it.

The blind, bland sanguinity of some merchants is staggering!

One thief paid an unsuspecting twelve-year-old boy a dollar to cash a stolen check for him in a grocery store.

"Did the government send you this check?" asked the grocery clerk of the boy.

"Yes," the innocent child said, not really comprehending the question.

"Okay," said the clerk and blithely handed over the cash without even knowing who the boy was.

This mad conversation and scene becomes almost totally incredible when one discovers that the check the boy handed the clerk bore the legend for all to see: "Old Age and Survivors' Insurance"!

Another instance, equally baffling: A chain store grocery

manager in New York City cashed a *negative photostatic copy* of a U.S. Government check! "Even if it had been a positive photostat," the Secret Service agent on the case wrote to me, "the store manager's gullibility would be hard to credit. The fact that it was a negative makes it almost impossible to believe. Yet it was true."

Stealing and cashing government checks became so easy that in time whole gangs began to enter the field. During my tenure as Chief some of these operations became highly organized and very difficult to break up.

One gang which formed in Georgia in 1957 was typical. It worked with absolute discipline and with a hierarchical system of authority proceeding downward from its youthful head man, one Edward Hunter, a brilliant organizer and leader whose talents deserved a better fate than those he put them to.

The gang had a regular promotion system. Hunter started his recruits out as thieves, lifting checks from mailboxes and aiming to fill prearranged quotas without getting arrested. The next highest group in the hierarchy made surveys to find apartment houses at which the delivery of government checks was greatest. Next highest in rank were those who prepared false identification; next, those who forged endorsements. And then—at the pinnacle—there were those who got the checks cashed.

Catching this group presented great difficulties, for their finesse got them out of harm's way in most cases before we could catch up with them. Hunter had stolen hundreds of automobile license blanks and, since most merchants consider licenses the ultimate in identification, the gang did not have much trouble in passing their checks. To make assurance doubly sure, however, every passer was followed by a "watcher" after he entered a store. The watcher ignored the passer, pretending not to be with him. However, if the manager or clerk seemed to hesitate over the identification the watcher would come up to the counter and with a display of surprise suddenly recognize the passer and call him by the name on the check. This almost always convinced the storekeeper that the identification was in order.

We needed the close co-operation of merchants to apprehend this gang. What we were up against, however, is illustrated by the following tale of ultimate carelessness by one merchant victim.

On this occasion Hunter sent four gang members out together to cash five checks each. They traveled to Columbus, Georgia, and, one by one, entered a liquor store there, each cashing one check. They then congregated at a near-by saloon and merely swapped hats. Then each one repaired to the liquor store and went to *the same clerk*. He promptly cashed another check for them. Next they swapped coats and went through the performance with the same clerk, again successfully. Next they swapped ties, and, on the fifth try, shirts, and each time the same clerk cashed their checks for them unquestioningly.

Even the crooks were impressed by this fellow. When they were arrested they referred to him as "the blind bunny."

It took us months before we could educate the merchants this gang preyed upon to give us the co-operation we needed. By careful investigation we had pieced together its habits, descriptions of some of the passers and the techniques they used for identification. At last we got a break; a merchant recognized one of the gang and was able to collar the suspect. His arrest led directly to Hunter and the rest.

The batting average of the Secret Service with check stealers, as with counterfeiters, has been almost 100 per cent. This iron fact has not, however, discouraged the hope that springs eternal in the breast of the small-time recidivist and I feel that this modern-day crime is here to stay despite the fact that it calls for a prison term of up to ten years and almost certain conviction.

Another crime that has grown considerably in the past quarter-century has been the theft of U.S. Government bonds. Some crooks actually specialize in stealing and cashing these bonds, largely, I suppose, because so many people keep them at home, not realizing that crooks know more about secret cubbyholes and other likely hiding places than a law-abiding homeowner could think up in a decade.

Take "Funeral Ben," for example. He was a second-story man with a difference. It was his practice to read the obituary column in the city he happened to be in and then call on the family of one recently deceased. He was always careful, however, to time his call with the absence of the survivors at cemetery or funeral home. Funeral Ben had an encyclopedic grasp of possible hiding places and could ferret out bonds no matter where they were stored. He ignored jewelry and silver. Once he made a haul by discovering a hiding place behind a loose brick in an outdoor barbecue in a back yard. The owner was flabbergasted. "I never thought anybody would ever look there," he said.

An excellent forger, Funeral Ben got away with several thousands of dollars in savings bonds before we caught him.

The crime of stealing bonds is also, in my opinion, one that will be with us for some time. This is so because savings bond owners are not motivated to be particularly careful about their bonds. They know that an indulgent government will make good on them even if they are stolen.

We of the Secret Service are kept on the perpetual go not alone by the larceny of the criminal classes. Many ordinary citizens also contribute to the burning of our midnight oil.

Take the simple matter of making good on partially destroyed currency. It is our duty to investigate any suspicious claims from the public at large—and there are hosts of them. People are forever sending in parts of bills and trying to get the full amount back. Often they've simply torn a good bill in two parts and are trying to get the total face value twice. They never do.

The Treasury's rule of thumb is that if not less than three-fifths of a bill is destroyed you can get the whole amount. Howover, if you have less than three-fifths of the bill and can prove beyond doubt that the rest was accidentally destroyed you can also get the whole amount. I can tell you that it takes some proving in such a case. But even if you can't prove the note was destroyed accidentally and yet have between two-fifths and three-fifths you can get half of the full amount back.

The rule is necessary, for some mighty strange things happen to currency. One five-dollar bill was dropped in a steel rolling mill and was flattened out to twice its size. On another occasion a one-dollar bill was left in a milk bottle and put through a sterilizing process. It came out about one-third of its original size and George Washington looked as if he'd been captured by native head-hunters. Both of these bills were of course fully redeemable despite their ghastly experiences. Redeemable too was the five-dollar bill torn into a hundred pieces by an insane woman; when she recovered she pieced it together and we had to pay.

However, unredeemable was the production of a "clever" bank teller—he got nothing for his considerable pains but criminal prosecution. He sent in sixteen pieces of a five-hundred-dollar bill—well over the two-thirds required for full payment. We were suspicious, however, and were able to prove that the pieces were parts of sixteen different five-hundred-dollar bills the clerk had snipped pieces from.

Here's a case I found both puzzling and fascinating.

Not long ago a bank in Albany, New York, acting for an unidentified customer, sent the Treasury Department redeemable portions of three hundred-dollar bills. These the department promptly redeemed.

Later the same month a CPA in New York City sent in the other portions of the *same* three hundred-dollar bills. The edges of these bills were slightly charred. The CPA stated that he owned the money and had put the bills in an envelope; that his five-year-old nephew had found the envelope and had burned it, with the present (enclosed) results.

The CPA was promptly visited in New York City by a Secret Service agent and when discrepancies in his story about his nephew appeared he admitted the bills might not have been burned by the little boy after all but might have been burned in the glove compartment of his car. The envelope had been there, he said, and the car had been stolen and demolished by two thieves, one of whom had been killed and the other seriously hurt. It turned out that his car had indeed been stolen and had been wrecked but there had been no fire in it.

We were now thoroughly puzzled and shifted our attention to Albany. Our agents found out that the bank there had been acting for an individual who had retrieved the other three redeemable portions of the hundred-dollar bills from a bartender. This latter in turn had received the mutilated bills from the owner of the restaurant. The bartender and his friend had agreed they'd split the proceeds if the notes could be redeemed; and redeem them they had, as I've stated.

Further investigation revealed that a girl who hung out in the bar had originally gotten the portions of three hundred-dollar bills from a New York City man who had been in Albany for the night and had gone out on a drinking spree. He had torn the bills in half and told the woman how she could get the other halves. She thought the matter over and later gave her halves to the restaurant owner.

Now we set about the task of finding out who the heavy drinker had been. The trail finally led to a New York City advertising executive who'd been in Albany for a convention. He had wakened the next morning with a hangover. Later he had turned over the three parts of the bills to his accountant to see if they could be redeemed.

Confronted with this story the accountant still denied he had deliberately charred the bills. However, we didn't believe him and the grand jury didn't either.

Another type of larcenist the Secret Service must cope with constantly is the violator of our gold laws. Every trick in the book is tried by gentlemen of this calling. Not long ago a smuggler attempted to get gold out of the United States by having the contraband metal melted down and shaped into automobile fenders. These he attached to his car and painted them over. His plan was to take his car to Europe with him.

We nailed him at Customs. The gold had made his standard-brand car suspiciously heavy when it was routinely weighed in during customs inspection. A customs agent then noted a slight bulge in the fenders, scratched the paint on one of them with his tie clasp and the golden jig was up.

Another new illegal gambit with gold was tried by two thieves on the West Coast in the latter part of 1957. These gentle grafters would steal gold ornaments and jewelry, melt them down and sell the gold. They claimed their precious product came from placer mining they did in the hills. It turned out they owned a mine all right, but it was only a front. The gold they sold didn't come from it. When, on a tip, we arrested them we put their product through a very up-to-the-minute chemical test which proved conclusively that it had been through a refining process before; thus it couldn't have come directly from their mine as they had held. Confronted with our findings they confessed their subterfuge and their crimes.

The United States Bureau of Engraving and Printing, the place where all our paper currency is made, must be constantly guarded against theft. No crook in his right mind would try to attack this great money factory from the outside, but every once in a while somebody on the inside gets an idea it can be breached.

Not too long ago one James Landis, a young Negro clerk in the Bureau, managed to get out of the building with $128,-

ooo in newly printed twenty-dollar bills cleverly concealed on his person. So far, so good. But then, believing that as soon as the Secret Service discovered the theft, it would circularize the serial numbers on the bills, he started on one of the biggest spending sprees in Washington's history. His object, of course, was to change the stolen bills into untraceable cash.

To help him he enlisted the aid of two young cronies, Roger Patterson and Charles Nelson. The three of them, their pockets bulging with thousands of dollars' worth of twenties, now roamed the streets buying everything in sight and getting change for their purchases. They bought cars, radios, television sets, toilet supplies, clothes, clocks, watches, etc., not excluding whiskey.

They hid the goods they had bought and drank the whiskey. This latter action lent new color to their spending, gave them ideas. Now they got up a massive crap game and poured their money into it, sometimes staking the players with rolls of twenties and thus betting against their own money.

Five days went by before we were able to catch up with them. In that time they were able to establish new records in spree spending. In all, I have figured, they were able to change about $26,000 into smaller bills within five days. In doing so the three young men garnered epic hangovers.

The solution of the case was a policeman's dream of happy coincidence. A conscience-stricken uncle of Landis had been let in on the illegal windfall. A good man, he couldn't stand to see his young nephew go down the drain. He phoned us, and told us all, "for my nephew's good."

It may well have been, too. From all probation reports it would seem that young Landis may go straight in the future.

I sincerely hope so, for, aside from this one wrong deed, he is a promising and likable young fellow.

These, then, are a few of the things which, sandwiched between protecting the President and catching the counterfeiter, we busy ourselves with in the Secret Service. They tend to keep our days, and often our nights too, rather crowded.

chapter 16

Another Kind of Assassin

A THOUSAND ITEMS CROWD IN ON ME AND I WISH I had room to tell them all, for they reveal, in general, much of the real relationship, the day-to-day working relationship, between the First Family and the Secret Service.

Here, for example, is a homely and innocent little item that happened on the morning of May 8, 1953. Mrs. Eisenhower pushed the buzzer that lies by her bed at about 2 A.M. on that date. She wished to summon the White House usher. However, he goes off duty at midnight and so the Secret Service agent on duty responded. Mrs. Eisenhower's window, it seems, had become stuck while it was up and the rain had started to pour down and was coming in. And she had become a little frantic the way any housewife might get if she saw the water sluicing in on her nice white curtains. Almost six million dollars for renovation, I remember reflecting wryly when the report came to me of the incident, and the windows still stick.

Another item, a little less innocuous, which concerned Mrs. Eisenhower: When leaving a friend's apartment on Connecticut Avenue with her mother, Mrs. John Doud, the two entered an elevator which immediately began to fall, drifting down fairly slowly, with its door open. Mrs. Eisenhower jumped out at the second floor and escaped unscathed but Mrs. Doud wrenched her knee while trying to get off. The elevator was checked out and the diagnosis, "relay trouble in the circuit," was made. To know what happened after the event was cold comfort. But I could not blame myself too much, for at the social pace the Eisenhowers maintained at this point, it would have been impossible to check all the elevators members of the family used every time they went out. Excepting the President's elevators, of course; these were always prechecked.

The Eisenhowers transformed social life in Washington. They loved to entertain, to give receptions, teas and parties, both formal and informal. To my mind the contrast between Mamie Eisenhower and Bess Truman was marked mainly by their attitudes toward such social occasions. While Mrs. Truman was a warm and charming person she did not entertain nearly so often as Mrs. Eisenhower did. She seemed to enjoy herself most with a few close friends, though she was at all times an excellent hostess. Mrs. Eisenhower, on the other hand, reveled in parties, loved the gay and informal ones as well as the formal ones. Party-lovers perked up considerably when the Eisenhowers entered the White House.

Indeed, even my wife and I were gradually initiated into Washington's new social life. As Chief of the Secret Service my name went into the famous Green Book, the Social Register of the District of Columbia—and we were invited to many of the exclusive parties, sometimes even to goings-on at the White House. It was at first very exciting. My head was not turned, however, I am happy to state. Friendships made in Washington, I gradually noticed, remain, with a few exceptions, basically cool and impersonal. I suppose this is due to the transiency of many government jobs but perhaps it can also be partially ascribed to the underlying coldness of the "career personality," as my wife and I began to call certain types of individuals we met.

It was during this period that truly vicious rumors began to spread about Mrs. Eisenhower. These sprang from the fact that sometimes when she had to stand for some time, say in a reception line, she would stagger. The things people said to account for these symptoms were totally unforgivable. I know for a fact that Mrs. Eisenhower had a condition which caused her to suffer from vertigo. This was, on occasion, very severe and if someone was not on hand to catch her she would actually fall. I have a written diagnosis of her condition from a physician. He described it as "a disturbed motor metabolism of the inner ear." The Secret Service agents who guarded Mrs. Eisenhower always saw to it that she had something to lean against when she was in the reception line, the back of a chair or the edge of a table.

Glancing over my diary at this point I see that I have noted several items that again show the day-to-day scope and detail of Secret Service duties. Here are a few.

ITEM: There were threats that the Eisenhower grandchildren would be harmed. These came in as phone calls during the famous death watch for the Rosenbergs, the husband and wife who were executed for espionage. I doubled the guard on the children, but nothing happened.

ITEM: Routine investigation by the Secret Service showed that a job applicant for a clerkship at the White House had been a call girl in Miami. P.S. She did not get the job. The official report said she'd been turned down on grounds of emotional instability, which to my mind was the understatement of the season.

ITEM: Horrid and obscene pictures showing photographs of the faces of famous women glued onto nudes in lewd postures suddenly appeared. Queen Elizabeth and Princess Margaret and other women, including the First Lady and Mrs. Barbara Eisenhower, were lampooned in this disgusting manner. It was clearly a security matter for the Secret Service, for anybody so mentally sick as to do this might also kill. An investigation was launched and we traced the source to a degenerate in Baltimore. He was given a psychiatric examination and put in a mental hospital—but fast!

ITEM: Threats from psychotics against the First Family and visits to the White House by such individuals increased twofold before Mr. Eisenhower's heart attack. Selecting at random from our callers during this period I see that one pleasant-faced young man informed the agent on duty at the northwest gate of the White House that he was assuming the Presidency of the United States and would review the troops on the White House lawn in fifteen minutes. . . . Another begged to have the President simply show himself. He told the guard that he was convinced that Mr. Eisenhower had become totally invisible and he wished us to convince him that the President was still flesh and blood. We searched him and found a long, curved knife on him. . . . A lady who was going the rounds with others to see the state rooms in the White House managed to set several small fires before she was discovered. Luckily not much damage was done and she was carted off to the place where she belonged. . . . Still another uninvited caller came to the northwest gate of the White House with a wildly hallucinatory complaint—that Bing Crosby and Bob Hope were sexually assaulting her nightly. "I don't know how they get into my room," she told the Secret Service agents who interviewed her. "They're terribly ingenious." She was of course sent to the hospital for observation.

ITEM: I received a call from the Secret Service bomb detail that there was a hand grenade on the White House lawn. A gardener had found it while mowing. I got right over there and the bomb detail soon discovered it was a dud. Some insane person had simply lobbed it over the fence. In this case, however, we never did catch the culprit, and that fact made me uneasy for a while.

ITEM: President Eisenhower told me that he had to lean out of his limousine window to wave to people and that this not only tired him but, when it was raining out, he got drenched. He himself suggested that possibly a Plexiglas top could be made so that he could see and be seen more easily. I put the problem up to the Ford Company and they came up with the famous Bubbletop.

[209]

ITEM: I went fishing with the President. The formality when one goes fishing with most Presidents is to catch less than they do—but you didn't have to observe that with Mr. Eisenhower. He is one of the best fishermen I've ever seen and could hit a lily pad at a hundred feet with a trout rod and light line. His catch was double mine and I was trying hard.

ITEM: A special putting green was constructed on the rear lawn of the Presidential residence. The White House squirrels started digging up this green and the White House Police decided to transport the squirrels to other areas. A news item on this forced migration appeared and a flood of letters descended from all parts of the country. The indignation aroused had hardly been equaled since the firing on Fort Sumter—the starvation of little children in the Congo made barely a ripple in comparison. All the time of course the President's health, perhaps chiefly maintained by his golf (if I read Dr. Paul Dudley White correctly), was pointing toward that dreadful time so soon to arrive.

ITEM: The President received a fine gift from a firearms company. It was a beautiful replica of an early model of a gun famous in our history. Presumably it was safe to shoot, coming as it did from the officers of the company, but I took no chances. I had it checked and found it would have probably blown up in the President's hand, possibly killing him, if he had shot it.

And now the biggest item of all—the heart attack and the awful time of suspense that followed:

As you may recall, there was a very close and warm friendship between the President and his wife's mother, Mrs. John Doud. He and his wife loved to visit her in her home at 750

Lafayette Street in Denver, Colorado. In fact, these visits soon became so customary that we had set up a miniature White House at Lowry Air Force Base in Denver, with an office for the President and quarters for the Presidential party.

On the occasion of the President's visit to Denver in the fall of 1955 I did not accompany him for I was involved with two big counterfeiting cases that had suddenly struck. The first time I heard of the illness was over my short-wave radio on my way home. It said the President had had a digestive attack and was resting comfortably. I whizzed back to the office and contacted Jim Rowley, who was of course in Denver with the White House Detail. From then on I stayed in constant touch with him, but I did not go right out to Denver for we did not wish to give the impression that any of us around the President expected the worst.

Rowley filled me in. He had been aroused from sleep by a phone call from the President's physician, Major General Howard Snyder, at 6:20 that morning and asked to stand by, the President wasn't feeling well. At 8:00 A.M. Murray Snyder, Jim Hagerty's assistant, announced that the President was indisposed and wouldn't go to work that day. Newspapermen, who thought Eisenhower was coming to work later in the day, remained, for the most part, at Lowry Field. Thus, when Dr. Snyder called for the Secret Service to take the President to the hospital that day, the agents took him directly out the front door to his destination, Fitzsimmons Hospital.

What was the course of the President's illness? What kind of medical care does a President get? Does it differ from yours and mine? What actually happens in the sick room and in the hospital minute by minute, hour by hour when a President of the United States becomes an emergency patient? We get intimations of answers to such questions from the newspapers but the best running account I know of, giving details which are often homely and minute, are in the bulletins my agents sent me daily. Here you can see exactly the kind of information the Chief of the Secret Service gets by special teletype or by special mail from his men in the field during a crisis. These bulletins are no longer "classified" and I am going to publish parts of them herewith. In the first bulletin I was told of the beginning of the President's illness and of the evasion of the press. Here is the second dispatch sent to me.

U.S. Secret Service
September 26, 1955

CHIEF—WASHINGTON
SUPERVISING AGENT—DENVER WHITE HOUSE

The events of Saturday, September 24, involving the activities of the President. [Continued from previous account of evasion of press and the secret movement of the President to Fitzsimmons Hospital.]

BULLETIN 2:

We drove to the rear entrance of the main hospital building. The President was assisted out of the car and supported to a wheel chair and wheeled ten feet to the elevator which ascended to the 8th floor, the tower part of the hospital, where he was wheeled to room 8002 and immediately placed in bed under an oxygen tent. After the President was settled, Dr. Snyder informed the writer that at 2:30 A.M. this morning he was summoned by Mrs. Eisenhower and that on his arrival his examination of the President showed the President's condition as a coronary thrombosis attack, anterior type.

Dr. Snyder also advised that the President would, at a minimum, have to remain in the hospital three weeks and perhaps longer. Therefore, the following action was taken with a view of establishing posts for this period as well as other associated plans. It was determined, on an inspection, that there were three rooms on this floor, the room presently occupied by the President, Room 8021 which is assigned to the First Lady and is located at the opposite corner from that of the President's, room 8016 assigned to Dr. Snyder, a dining room, a reception room presently occupied by the agents and a pantry located at the opposite end of the corridor to the President's room. There are two elevators servicing these floors as well as a rear elevator. There is a large assembly room opposite the rear elevator where the physicians at the hospital hold their conferences. However their conferences will be discontinued during the time the President is on this floor. Now, it will be converted into an office for Col. Robert L. Schulz [the President's aide].

The kind of detail given here allowed me to assess the situation as it developed and to plan matters concerning the President's protection while at the hospital with some intelligence. But let us go on with the report for one can get a close-up and dispassionate view of the factors involved best in this way.

7:30 P.M. The First Lady accompanied by Colonel Schulz arrived at the hospital via the rear entrance and was met by Major General Martin E. Griffin and escorted to her room on the 8th floor.

8:00 P.M. A second cardiograph was made of the President.

12:10 A.M. Mr. Hagerty and Dr. T. W. Mattingly, heart specialist at Walter Reed Hospital, arrived from Washington, D.C. They immediately went into consultation with Drs. Snyder and Pollock, after which they went in and examined the President.

12:52 A.M. The consultation concluded. Mr. Hagerty then departed to issue his first press release to the waiting press. There is set herein below the names of the physicians, nurses and technicians who have been assigned to attend the President over each 24 hour period.

As you can see, a White House in miniature immediately forms around a President wherever he may happen to be. The Secret Service report for this day further detailed for me how the agents had developed a telephonic system I had ordered for this hospital White House, how the supervising agent had stationed the other agents in depth in and around the hospital to protect the President, how a method for examining mail and X-raying potentially dangerous packages had been set up just as if the President were in Washington. I was informed of the arrangements to have Dr. Paul Dudley White, the famous heart specialist, flown from Boston to Denver and of the periodic examinations of Mr. Eisenhower which were continued.

The third bulletin I received reflected the fact that the impromptu White House set up by the Secret Service men and other aides was already functioning smoothly—twenty-four hours later.

U.S. Secret Service
September 27, 1955

CHIEF—WASHINGTON
SUPERVISING AGENT—DENVER WHITE HOUSE

The activities at the hospital for Monday, September 26, 1955.

7:40 A.M. After a restful night the President had breakfast, consisting of prunes, oatmeal, a soft-boiled egg, toast and a glass of milk.

8:40 A.M. A cardiograph was taken by Sgt. Killian [a technician at the hospital] during which time the following were in consultation: Drs. White, Mattingly, Pollock and Howard Snyder.

9:45 A.M. Dr. White in company with Secretary Hagerty and Dr. Howard Snyder . . . departed the hospital en route to Lowry Air Force Base where Dr. White addressed the press conference, explaining the President's condition by giving a dissertation on coronary thrombosis. He indicated it would be two weeks from the time of the attack before the President's scar would commence to heal and another two weeks of quiet at the hospital and a month of convalescing. Thereafter it is expected that the President will be able to carry on his normal work.

1:05 P.M. Luncheon was served the President, consisting of ham, two slices of bread, fresh fruit salad, lettuce and tomato salad and a glass of milk.

4:00 P.M. Another cardiograph was taken by Sgt. Killian with Dr. Pollock present.

4:30 P.M. Colonel Schulz, at the request of the President, installed a telex earphone to enable the President to listen to musical recordings.

6:15 P.M. Dinner was served to the President consisting of a piece of roast beef, one slice of bread, baked tomato, beets, spinach, fresh fruit cup and a glass of milk.

6:20 P.M. Lieutenant Colonel John Eisenhower returned to the hospital after attending Mr. Hagerty's press conference and visiting his grandmother at 750 Lafayette Street. Special Agent Flohr drove him to these places and return.

7:15 P.M. Drs. Mattingly and Pollock checked the President's blood pressure, etc. During the course of the day the oxygen tent was withdrawn on three occasions for 30 minute periods.

REMARKS: The First Lady and Lieutenant Colonel John, during the course of the day and particularly at meal times, visited with the President. He had a restful night, sleeping continuously from 8:00 P.M. until 6:00 this morning, Tuesday, September 27th.

These reports continued throughout the President's illness and, indeed, as he recovered and more people were allowed to visit him they became enormously detailed.

This amount of detail was my doing. I had instructed my men to record the name of every person who entered and left the President's room or the eighth floor of the hospital.

I had my reason for initiating this cumbersome and boring routine. Ugly rumors had followed hard on the deaths of several Presidents, notably those of Warren G. Harding and

Franklin D. Roosevelt. These rumors generally concerned mysterious personages who were supposed to have been seen entering or leaving the rooms of the dying Presidents shortly before they died. If President Eisenhower were to die, God forbid, I did not want his death sullied by such rumors. And thus our files are bulky for this period with reams of notations such as these:

At 3:35 P.M. Lt. Col. John Sheedy visited the President and set up a record player to play an album of Jackie Gleason records. He departed at 3:50. At 3:59 P.M. John Clark, electrician, visited the President's room with the Chief Nurse and departed at 4:01. At 4:13 P.M. Captain Prout replenished the recorder with new records and departed at 4:17 P.M. The President listened to western reading records from 4:15 P.M. until 4:40 P.M. At 4:26 P.M. Captain Prout visited the President's room and left at 4:28 P.M. At 4:36 P.M. the First Lady visited the President and left at 4:50 P.M.

On and on the list goes.

But the President was getting better and the new flock of visitors attested to that. When I thought it would cause no comment I went on to Denver myself and stayed until the President was well enough to return to Washington. I went to see him the moment I arrived and I thought he looked fine and felt very encouraged, but when I spoke to Mrs. Eisenhower she seemed to be still quite worried and this tempered my cheer. I went in after that to visit the President often and he always welcomed me; a more cheerful and thoughtful patient I have never seen.

One day Mr. Eisenhower told me: "I won't leave here, I've decided, until I can go on foot. That means I'll have to be able to walk up and down a flight of stairs." The wait wasn't so

long as some of us had feared. On November 11, 1955, I returned with him to Washington in the *Columbine,* his private
plane.

The President could get about but he had to take it very
easy for some time. Then, just as I felt he was really getting
his full strength back, fate struck him down again. This time
it was the attack of ileitis, and it occurred just a little over a
half a year after the coronary thrombosis.

When I heard the news I felt depressed indeed. As a lay-
man I could not see how he could survive this serious illness,
knowing what I knew about the condition of his heart and all
he had been through.

In telling this dramatic episode in the life of the President
I will again use the reportorial powers of my agents. In order
to give me the true facts they first obtained an "eyewitness"
account of the President's illness from the person who would
know most about it—Dr. Snyder. Here is an abridged account
of the President's attack from the first moment it occurred
right up to the emergency operation, as the President's personal physician gave it to my deputy.

Friday, June 8, 1956:

12:45 A.M. I was retiring after having attended the White
House Photographers' Association Dinner when I was called by
Mrs. Eisenhower, who stated that the President, after about an
hour and a half sleep, said to her when he was aroused by her
coming to bed that he had a little discomfort in his abdomen.
Mrs. Eisenhower reported this to me over the telephone. I suggested trying a tablespoonful of Milk of Magnesia.

1:10 A.M. Mrs. Eisenhower called again and reported no improvement and said she had requested a car to pick me up. [A
Secret Service car, of course, for this was a matter of the President's welfare and safety. U.E.B.]

1:20 A.M. I arrived at the White House.

1:30 A.M. The President transferred to his bed in his dressing room. Blood pressure 140/100; pulse 94–100, considerable arrhythmia, heart sounds otherwise normal; temperature normal; respiration normal. He complained of pain in abdomen. No nausea. No heart burn. Upper abdomen tympanitic [inflated, distended]. Abdomen not distended. No particular point of tenderness. No shock. Extremities warm. Quinidine Sulfate, three grains, administered . . .

2:15 A.M. President slept quietly during this interval. Breathing normal and quiet . . . Complained of discomfort in lower abdomen. No cramps or "colic." No nausea. No eructations. No desire to visit toilet. No point of definite tenderness. General soreness to the right and below the umbilicus above old abdominal scar.

3:45 A.M. The President slept, breathing quietly with mouth closed. Awoke still complaining of discomfort in lower abdomen. Blood pressure 140/100; pulse 90–96, arrhythmia, heart sounds otherwise normal; respiration 20; temperature 98.4. Moderate distention high in abdomen under diaphragm. No special point of tenderness, although he still complained of soreness on palpation over lower right abdomen. No nausea. Gas sounds in abdomen. Administered 15 cc. of Ararol. President returned to sleep and slept until 4:45 A.M.

4:45 A.M. President awoke complaining of same abdominal discomfort and soreness over the lower right abdomen. Blood pressure 136/96; pulse 88–92 . . .

5:15 A.M. Blood pressure 130/90 . . .

6:00 A.M. Blood pressure 126/84 [falling—U.E.B.]. . . . Abdominal discomfort not materially increased . . . Moderately increased distention of upper left abdomen. No evidence of shock. Extremities warm.

6:30 A.M. Blood pressure 112/80 [falling—U.E.B.].

7:40 A.M. Called Ann Whitman [President's appointment secretary] and asked to have appointments for the morning postponed. Said the President would not be in his office at least during the morning.

8:00 A.M. Blood pressure 110/80 [still falling—U.E.B.] . . .

Scalp and hands cool and moist. Abdominal discomfort has continued throughout with no marked increase either of discomfort or soreness . . . The soreness is general over the lower right quadrant, but more pronounced over upper portion. Talked with Jim Hagerty and told him he could announce that the President had an upset stomach.

8:15 A.M. Saw Hagerty and Governor Adams. Told them the President was not showing any signs of improvement.

8:40 A.M. Called Walter Reed Hospital to locate General Heaton [Major General Leonard Heaton, who is Commanding General at Walter Reed, an army hospital]. Was told that he was still on vacation in Virginia.

9:00 A.M. . . . Abdominal distention slightly increased about umbilicus and above to the left . . .

9:15 A.M. . . . On telephone with General Heaton. I told him I would make arrangements to have him returned by airplane . . . called Colonel Mattingly at home and learned he had left by automobile for Columbia, South Carolina at 5:00 A.M. this morning.

9:30 A.M. Heart sounds essentially normal.

9:40 A.M. No decrease in discomfort. Condition good, but abdominal distention increasing.

10:00 A.M. Called Walter Reed . . . to have ambulance ready for call.

10:30 A.M. Blood pressure 108/76 [still decreasing] and pulse 92 regular [increasing], heart sounds normal, respiration 20.

10:40 A.M. President slept.

10:50 A.M. Awakened by cramp in calf of right leg.

10:55 A.M. Drowsy. Complained of generalized abdominal discomfort. Distention centered about umbilicus and above to the left.

11:30 A.M. Blood pressure 106/86; pulse 96.

11:45 A.M. Blood pressure 106/84; pulse 100, regular, heart sounds normal but more rapid and not so forceful; respiration 20. Perspiring, noticeably hands and forehead. No generalized sweating . . . Called Jim Hagerty to office and notified him President had ileitis. Did not mention there was probably an obstruction.

[219]

11:55 A.M. . . . Intravenous glucose and water, 100 drops per minute, begun. [This was done to restore the President's blood chemistry which, by going out of balance, was causing his pulse to rise and his blood pressure to fall. Meanwhile the decision was made to remove the President to the hospital when the intravenous glucose had restored his blood balance. U.E.B.]

1:05 P.M. Blood pressure and pulse returning toward normal.

1:20 P.M. Intravenous discontinued.

1:25 P.M. President put on a stretcher. Carried to South Portico and placed in ambulance.

1:40 P.M. Arrived at Walter Reed. Removed President from ambulance and transferred him to suite in Ward 8. Learned that General Heaton had been picked up by airplane and will arrive about 2:15 P.M. Learned that Dr. Mattingly has been located and will be flown in from Columbia, South Carolina by jet plane.

2:15 P.M. General Heaton arrived. We immediately discussed the question of civilian consultants and decided upon leading men in this field: Drs. Brian Blades and John Lyons, both of Washington, and Dr. Isidor S. Ravdin of Philadelphia. General Heaton called Blades and Lyons. I called Ravdin. Located him at a meeting of the American Medical Association in Chicago. He stated he would take an airplane immediately and arrive as soon as possible.

Dr. Snyder's dramatic account ends at this point. The prominent specialists he mentioned, and whom he had summoned, soon began to arrive and when they were all there they went into a conclave to decide whether or not to operate. The meeting lasted for hours, with constant referral to the President's chart and his current condition. It was not till two the next morning that the final decision was made. It was—an emergency operation, at once.

Things now really began to move. I return you to the log kept by my supervising agent to give a view of the dramatic procedure.

2:05 A.M. The President was lifted from his bed and placed on a litter.

2:07 A.M. The President was rolled on the litter from his room to the Operating Room #6 on the Third Floor.

2:09 A.M. The President was lifted from the litter and placed on the operating table. At this point I listed the times and procedures in the preparation and operation of the President:

2:25 A.M. Anesthesia induction started . . .

2:59 A.M. Skin incision. They reached the region of the ileitis [the smaller intestines] where they found a thickening of an old scar blocking the bowel [the obstruction Dr. Snyder had noted], whereupon they decided to do a short circuit operation [that is, they decided to cut the "blocked" part right out and hitch up the two ends. It's called an anastomosis].

3:58 A.M. Anastomosis complete.

4:25 A.M. The operation was completed successfully. The President's condition was good, without complications. When the President was returned to his room he was still under anesthesia, but at 8:00 A.M. there was a satisfactory reaction from it and the usual pertinent post-operative supportive measures were then instituted and the President rested throughout the day.

Thus ends this marvelously circumstantial account of the President's two major illnesses. Both the coronary thrombosis and the ileitis attack had happy endings. However, they were to change the President drastically as a human being.

When the very first news of the heart attack had reached me I had immediately put a special guard around the Vice President. And I had done the same when news of the ileitis reached me. Now, however, as the passing of the weeks showed the President growing healthier by the day, I reduced Mr. Nixon's guard. He, for one, was very glad of it, and you shall presently see why.

chapter 17

Ike's Travels

THE PRESIDENT RECOVERED FROM HIS ILLNESSES
and then *I* was laid low—with a double hernia. I had to be
operated on and I spent six weeks convalescing, the longest
vacation I'd ever had in my life up till then. The day I got
back to work I went to the President's office on business and
he shook my hand and looked at me understandingly. "When
they cut into you with that knife, U.E.," he said to me ear-
nestly, "it really takes something out of you, doesn't it?" I had
to agree. "I hope they haven't clipped our wings forever," he
said.

They certainly hadn't clipped his. For, as soon as he'd recovered some of his strength, he'd decided to run for the

Presidency again—and he had the stamina to win it by a whacking majority. During this second term he became the most traveled President in U.S. history, covering over 100,000 miles in foreign countries and poking into every cranny of the world.

I know that Mr. Eisenhower felt that his single motive in all the traveling that he now decided to engage in was his desire to shore up the free world, to turn back anti-Americanism by selling our democratic message in person. I think myself, however, that he had another motive, without quite realizing it.

I had observed that, when he'd returned to work after his illnesses, he was far more active and restless than he'd ever been before. He seemed to be always on the go and seemed to chafe at being penned up in the White House. At least one doctor I know states that this kind of restlessness often follows a recovery from a coronary attack, though he wasn't certain whether this was some physical aftermath of the illness or the result of the "blood-thinning" medicine people who've had coronaries must take to guard against getting a blood clot.

To carry his message of democracy and to allay his restlessness, then, the President made four basic trips to break all records for Presidential travel abroad. They were, in order: his journey to West Germany, Great Britain and France; his tour of eleven nations in Asia, Europe, the Middle East and Africa; and, in the last year of his office, his travels to South America; and then to the Far East. Too, there were the trips that we had laid advance plans for but which never came off— the trip to Russia and the Japanese trip, both of which were canceled for urgent political reasons.

[223]

The Secret Service throughout the years had developed many techniques for protecting the President while he traveled. But it was during this vast flurry of comings and goings that, in my opinion, we brought all of our know-how to its full perfection and introduced some radical new methods. From the days when Teddy Roosevelt had been criticized for "violating the Constitution" by traveling to the Panama Canal Zone, the concept of a President's duties had changed considerably—but no more so than the techniques the Secret Service used to protect him.

Getting a President launched on a trip, even a short one, is a highly ramified job; for a long, foreign trip it's almost an infinitely ramified one. Even in this jet age, when every place is just a few hours away, Presidential trips mean huge amounts of advance paper work to be done, plans to be made. Protocol and diplomatic experts as well as a bevy of topflight Secret Service agents must go in advance and lay the groundwork for these trips, working out, step by step, minute by minute, every move the President will make.

Take the trip to India for example. Mr. Eisenhower was only going to stay there for five days. But I had six agents in New Delhi for a whole month before the President arrived, making what I called "a joint protective survey." These men reported back to me on every aspect of the plans for the President, including the nineteen different places he would sleep, eat and speak. All the plans made for the President's safety in each of these places had to be made with, and receive the approval of, eight branches of the Indian Government, such as the state and city police, the army, the foreign office, etc. In the end I had detailed maps and reports on every inch of the President's routes for every day and the disposition of all the protective forces we'd use and how they changed and shifted from one situation to the other.

A Secret Service function that has been brought to a high degree of perfection is our so-called "audio-visual security." This phrase refers to our techniques for making certain that nobody can tap in on the President while he's in his private quarters. We've used considerable ingenuity in devising these techniques and brought them to a high polish during the last years of the Eisenhower era.

When the advance agents had selected a residence for Mr. Eisenhower in a country he was to visit I would then send over our specially trained audio-visual crew to check the place for hidden recording devices or microphones. First thing they did was to take everything apart that could be taken apart in the entire living area. Every single book was taken down and looked through—books, carefully hollowed out, make excellent places to hide electronic equipment. Toasters, clocks, radios, electric irons, gas and electric stoves were all disassembled to the point where they could be looked into. Desks and tables were examined for anything unusual about their construction. Floors, ceilings and walls were examined for tiny holes where small listening devices might have been inserted.

When all this had been done the men brought in our "basic search kit." This is a series of electronic devices we have put together for our special purposes; we have adapted them to help us discover whether any hidden instruments or techniques are being used to tap into the rooms.

The enemy is never to be underrated. When it comes to science he is often diabolically clever and we must overlook none of his tricks. He can, for example, put a rig on a regular electric outlet or a regular electrical wire in the wall that will conduct sound out of the President's living-quarters-to-be. Such a rig might go completely disregarded. But one of our electronic attachments can detect beyond any dispute whether the electrical wiring or outlets have been tampered with in this way. Another trick that can be used to listen in on the President is an ordinary telephone; this can be so tampered with that when the receiver is hung up the person at the other end can still hear—it does not disconnect. We have a special procedure that can detect whether this has been done to the President's phones.

Radio waves can be sent over television antennae and over intercom or ordinary electrical systems. Another special "listening to the listener" device tells us if such hidden devices are being used.

Still another machine we use is called an "electronic noise generator." When an agent turns this on, it has the capacity to make a hidden microphone start to hum loudly—which would of course lead us to it and allow us to render it *hors de combat.*

Another instrument in our basic search kit is called a metascope. This is a kind of tiny periscope with a light on the end of it. It's one of a medical doctor's basic instruments; he uses it to examine the dark innards of man. But we've adapted it. We can fit it into the tiniest hole we might find in a wall, a hole as small as the head of a match, and carefully scrutinize the area all around it for hidden instruments.

One of our most important machines is our portable X-ray. This is a very powerful machine and was specially designed for us. We use this to examine all gifts sent to the President while he is traveling—but we also use it in securing his rooms. If we find a desk or a chair that has an unusual structure or might have a false bottom we can use the machine to "see" whether any recording device, or even a bomb, might be concealed within it.

The advance experts must also determine whether the walls in the President's putative quarters are so constructed that ordinary listening devices, the type that magnifies sound, could pick up conversations from the outside. In places we found that if one talked too close to the walls he could be overheard but that he could not be heard from the center of the room. We then had to advise the President to do any private talking in the middle of the room.

When the walls of a room were too thin altogether and it wasn't safe even to talk in the middle room of the suggested quarters we would try to locate an alternate place for the President to live, or at least to hold conferences. If no place else was available we would commandeer quarters in our own embassy in the host country.

In addition to securing the President's living quarters we had, of course, to guard against poisoned food. The Russians, I had noted when Khrushchev visited here, were very careful about food, to the point where they checked everything Khrushchev ate with a Geiger counter. I think they were particularly sensitive about atomic dust, the story being that it may already have been used as a method of assassination in Russia.

I did not have a Geiger counter used for the President's food. I had decided early in Mr. Eisenhower's travels that it would be much safer if we had him eat just about what everybody else in his party ate while abroad. My logic was that if special food were prepared it would call attention to the eater.

But while the President ate what hoi polloi ate, I still had the advance agents very carefully check up on all kitchen personnel in the places he was to eat. The only special demands we made on foreign waiters, however, was that they should serve special spring water with the President's meals instead of the *eau du pays*. This was no great demand, for the President always had bottled spring water served to him in the White House.

The preparation of food for Mr. Eisenhower's plane while en route was another detail taken care of by the Secret Service agents I sent out in advance. As a typical example of the arrangements that had to be made, in India meals were prepared in the kitchen of the Imperial Hotel. This preparation was supervised by Pan American World Airways. The Indian cooks, of course, could not possibly know which part of the meal would be eaten by the President and which by other passengers. That was the margin of safety I depended upon in the food area. As soon as everything was prepared we then put it under guard, sealed it in metal containers and transported it directly to the Presidential plane.

The Presidential planes of course were jet-powered by the time President Eisenhower had started on his major foreign travels. However, on occasion he would have to switch from a jet to the prop-powered *Columbine III*, his old plane, for a short hop. This happened during part of the South American tour and it illustrates a very important point about the men who protect the President—their ruthless placement of the President's safety before all other considerations.

In Chile it turned out that there was only one refueling tank that held the kind of high-octane gasoline used in the old Super Constellation the President had switched to. The Secret Service agent in charge felt, however, that this supply source could easily have been spotted by a potential assassin, as the only place where the Eisenhower plane *could* get gasoline. This agent hit on a foolproof if somewhat cold-blooded way of establishing that the gasoline was safe.

A regular commercial airline was scheduled for refueling just ahead of the *Columbine III*. The agent decided that this plane could be a guinea pig for the Presidential plane. He wrote the following "advance" advice to me on his method: "If nothing happens to the commercial flight . . . then the assumption will be that the gasoline is safe and of a quality acceptable for the use of Columbine III." This kind of reasoning is quite understandable in men who are prepared to intercept a bullet aimed at the President with their own bodies.

When I fully realized that the President was venturing the reputation of his entire regime, even its place in history, on the travels he planned, I decided I should go along with him on as many trips as I possibly could. This was very difficult to do because of the constant attention I had to give to other aspects of my job—particularly to the ever-proliferating check and bond forgeries and to the counterfeiting that had recently taken a new surge forward. But the fact that the President had been so ill, that the nations of the world were so disturbed, and that so much seemed staked on these missions to foreign lands all made me feel that I had better be in charge of our streamlined caravan whenever possible.

There were some very bad moments on the trips. Our greatest dangers came from friendly crowds, oddly enough. Secret Service advance agents, as I've explained, always worked out detailed protection from the crowds with the military and police of the country we were visiting. Roped-off areas, barricades and all such crowd-control methods were always prearranged in minute detail. Generally I had from twenty-five to fifty Secret Service agents around the President on these travels. The host country supplied the rest of the guard, which was disposed around the President in the most effective ways possible, the details of which had been settled by the advance agents with the police. Here's one example to show the numbers involved in this protection: On the President's visit to Rio de Janeiro the Presidential guard consisted of 2,500 members of the Brazilian Armed Forces, 800 Federal District Police and 150 Palace Guards. Those figures are pretty average for the guards generally put at our disposal.

Trouble came when the local gendarmerie refused to stick by the plans they had agreed on with the Secret Service. As an illustration, when the President visited Acapulco there were terrific crowds on the road from the airport to the Presidential residence. Suddenly a section of this crowd broke through the barricades on the sides of the road and started to close in on the Presidential automobile. I was in the lead car directly in front of the car which carried our President and the President of Mexico. I looked around for an explanation of the unexpected and dangerous surge and saw a Mexican colonel who had previously worked out security arrangements

with us behaving in a very strange manner. He was harangu-
ing the crowd as if to tell them to stay back but at the same
time he was motioning them forward. I asked my interpreter
who sat next to me what the colonel was saying and he told
me that he was shouting: "Come closer, come closer, and see
the two great Presidents at the same time. It is your last chance.
Come closer."

The huge crowd, now excited, began to push in fast and
became exceedingly dangerous. I ordered the Mexican driver,
through my interpreter, to drive from one side of the street
to another and thus push the crowd back. The maneuver
successfully cleared a path for the Presidential car and we all
got safely to the residence. You can imagine that I spoke my
mind to that colonel later, though what I told him cannot be
repeated here.

By all odds though, the largest crowds were in India. They
were not really crowds at all: they were vast oceans of humanity which were at times absolutely out of control and beat
against our dwarfed caravan in inundating waves. They are
impossible to imagine and were extremely frightening to see.

There was no such thing as real control of these seething
masses. Many of them were religiously inspired, believing that
being close to a great man would help their immortal souls in
the hereafter. And, they believed, the closer they could get to
President Eisenhower, the better.

The most frightening experience of all was on the Kitchener
Road which led from the Palam Airport to New Delhi, a distance of twelve miles and normally traversable, even at a
ceremonial pace, in, say, forty-five minutes. Prime Minister
Nehru accompanied Mr. Eisenhower on this terrible ride,

and he became both apprehensive and enraged at the crowd's behavior. We inched our way through this vast sea of sweating, screaming humanity. No barricades had been erected to hold the crowd back as we had arranged to have done. The Indian police went ahead and to the side of the autocade swinging their clubs at the heads of those who barred the way. Wild-looking faces surrounded us; great heavy bouquets and tons of flowers were thrown at Mr. Eisenhower, who tried to stand up and wave back. Once when he turned to bend over to say something to Mr. Nehru a wet, leaden-weighted bouquet struck him in the back of the neck. He had to keep his hands before his face to ward off these floral offerings.

Here is how Merriman Smith, the dean of White House reporters, who was along on this trip, described the melee in *A President's Odyssey* (Harper, 1961).

Behind the shield of his arm, Eisenhower looked out at a scene never before witnessed by an American chief executive, the mass adulation of India that almost killed with its kindness. Men, women and children, crushing against the cars of the President's motorcade in what approached mass hysteria, had poured into New Delhi for days by train and truck, in rough lorries and overloaded busses, by camel carts and thousands simply by foot. . . . True, the Indian government had encouraged and even facilitated the turnout. But also true, the people of India turned out in masses that no one foresaw. . . . Nehru was worried. He nibbled at his upper lip and stroked his chin, hunched down in the wild melee of flower blossoms and warily eying the intense young men in turbans and shirtsleeves leaning into the car to roar the Urdu welcome, *"Hind Eisenhower ki jai!"* (Hail Eisenhower!). . . . Lean, hard India police, turbans askew and their starched khaki shirts and shorts beginning to wilt with sweat, shouted and swung at the crowd with lathis, a slender wooden stick much like the old swagger stick of the American Marines. . . . Much of the time, the only light on the turbulent scene came from the ceremonial lantern bearers from small villages whose ancient beacons wobbled and sometimes disappeared in the rolling waves of humanity. . . . The officers swung with their clubs first at the shins, then at the heads. When swinging threats failed to work, the police flailed at any body target available.

On the rear of the car bearing the two leaders, deadly serious American Secret Service men clung awkwardly to the bumpers and trunk area in such a manner that any exuberant Indian who tried to climb in with Eisenhower and Nehru had first to broach the American security barrier, thin as it was.

One of the agents was bleeding noticeably about the hands as he warded off the backswing of the police clubs flashing dangerously close to the President.

Indians crushed to the front of the crowd used what English they knew in calling out to Eisenhower. Dusk had turned to night, but some of the Indians proudly shouted, "Good morning, Ike," and with all the smiling dignity possible under trying circumstances, Eisenhower replied, "And good morning to you, sir."

But the worst was yet to come. Our caravan had inched forward but now it stopped completely under an archway that proclaimed Ike as "The Prince of Peace." The crowd was now getting out of hand completely and I was certain that our President was going to be injured if not killed in the crush.

At this point Nehru himself stepped into the breach. He leaped from the car and gave those around him a screaming lecture on their manners. At first the surrounding noise drowned out his voice completely but in time he was able to make them listen and to shame them into falling back and after having been entrapped in that worshiping maelstrom for twenty minutes we were able to move on to our destination.

This wild reception on the Kitchener Road outside New

Delhi was, to my mind, the high point of success for Mr. Eisenhower's good-will tours. He himself was amazed and tremendously buoyed up by the fantastic reception he'd gotten and by the world-wide press coverage, for that afternoon had made headlines everywhere. It looked at that moment as if his personal popularity could, almost unaided, force an era of good will upon the world. I saw him that night and he was terribly excited. None of us had ever seen him in quite such an exhilarated mood before. He could not seem to stop talking about the crowds and was virtually buttonholing listeners to tell them about it.

I was glad he had that moment of absolute triumph for there were cruel, tragic moments ahead. His dream of a new kind of diplomacy-through-popularity was destined to be shattered completely by the cancellation of his trips to Russia and Japan. The cynical men who engineered these final failures succeeded in making the end of his regime seem hollow and pathetic and futile.

But there were many exciting, disturbing and humorous moments before this sad conclusion.

There was the trip to England and Scotland and the awful ribbing the Secret Service took from the English press, for example.

Scotland Yard does not find it necessary to guard its King, Queen and Prime Minister the way we guard our President and his family. The English people, unlike us, are homogeneous and their feeling toward their rulers is such that an assassination attempt is, apparently, even beyond the imagination of their insane. Unless, of course, they've just been plain lucky so far, in which case I hope that their luck continues.

At any rate they find our elaborate precautions, our checking and planning and guarding, prime material for irony and ridicule.

Actually we might have escaped with a few minor jibes in the papers if it hadn't been for, of all people, James Hagerty, Mr. Eisenhower's own Press Secretary. When the Presidential party had just arrived in England and we were going through the English Customs at London Airport, Hagerty suddenly called out in a loud voice, to one of our senior agents, John Campion, "Campion, come over here." Campion complied and was questioned by a customs officer about the firearms he and the other agents were carrying with them. Naturally Campion told the truth, stating just what guns we had on our persons and what other weapons we were carrying. This was all right and had been arranged for but it so happened that English journalists were standing around twelve deep, as it were, listening to the interrogation. Mr. Hagerty should have known this and that they would jump on this material and exploit it for news. He should have taken Campion and the official into a separate room, not arranged the conference in such a public place.

We were not only jumped on journalistically, we were trod up and down upon, called every name under the sun. And fun was poked at us mercilessly. The entire press refused to refer to us as Secret Service agents but called us "pistol-toting G-men," "American tough guys" and made us out to be rough characters indeed.

We also ran into difficulties with the Queen's Equerry, the man who arranged her social programs. Perhaps put off by our poor publicity he absolutely refused to let our men accompany the President when he went to Balmoral Castle to visit the Queen. Finally we pointed out to Mr. Equerry (I have, strangely, forgotten his name though I usually have a very good memory for equerries) that our President had already had one heart attack and could just possibly have another. Wouldn't it be embarrassing if this should happen with nobody else around other than Englishmen? They would then have to explain why the President's guard had not been there, with the oxygen mask we carried and other first-aid supplies.

The Equerry saw our point finally and agreed to let the agents onto the grounds at Balmoral "if we kept out of sight of the Queen."

We had to agree to this "humiliating" condition for guarding our President. But I had a kind of Pyrrhic victory over Mr. Equerry in the end and I am small enough to say I enjoyed it. The Queen gave a picnic for Mr. Eisenhower on the grounds at Balmoral and we had to stay in a little shack in order to remain out of the royal eyesight.

The Queen, who was five months pregnant, appeared in slacks and I was slightly astonished at this informality on her part. But my "revenge" on Mr. Equerry came when Princess Margaret learned of the banishment of the American Secret Service and came over to our shack, entered it and introduced herself, saying, "My name is Margaret." She really is a great beauty and infinitely gracious. She stayed on and chatted with us and then Prince Philip walked over and she introduced him to us. We all had a very pleasant interlude for a half-hour or more. Later, when the Queen paid a visit to Washington I saw Philip at a reception and he looked at me for a long time and then said: "Haven't I seen you someplace before?"

"You sure have, Your Highness," I retorted laughingly, and I reminded him of the occasion. He laughed, too, and said, "Oh, yes, that was a jolly good time, a *jolly* good time." I am sure that both Margaret and Philip felt that the Equerry had been a bit overzealous, to say the least.

As a matter of fact, protocol-minded gentlemen such as the Queen's Equerry often caused the Secret Service difficulty. They are sometimes deeply insensitive men who seem to care far more for good form than for anything or anybody in the world. They nearly always seem to put ancient pomp and ceremony before the safety and security of the great men they serve.

In Greece, Italy and Spain these men dominated the situation pretty much. In Greece, for example, our advance agents, with the aid of the American Ambassador, had extracted a promise from the Greek protocol division to let our Secret Service car follow immediately behind the Presidential car in the motorcade from the airport to Athens. But the protocol men loved the ancient custom of surrounding the King's car with the Royal Horse. And, despite their promises to us, when the parade had formed there were the colorful mounted guard behind the car which carried Mr. Eisenhower and their monarch.

This may seem trivial enough but the Secret Service knows from experience that a car directly behind the President may save his life in certain emergencies. My point is that the protocol men were so blinded by their own worship of empty ceremony that they would risk the very lives of those they serve.

Nothing untoward happened that day, as good luck would have it. But during the months and years of the Presidential travels I had many, many bad moments, some funny ones, some sad.

I think for pure terror my worst moment occurred during a parade in Casablanca. I was in the lead car as usual; the President's car followed just behind. Suddenly our motorcade moved into a section of street which was lined on either side by huge black-bearded, wild-looking men on horseback carrying rifles. They had on long flowing white robes and turbans and seemed like something out of *The Arabian Nights*. Even as I looked my hair stood on end for suddenly they raised their rifles and pointed them what seemed to me to be directly at the President's car. And then they fired!

Fortunately, my interpreter was sitting next to me. Hastily he explained that these were Berber tribesmen and that their guns had no shot in them, just powder. Firing blanks above the head of their sovereign was the traditional Berber way of paying homage. The firing continued for a few miles. I think it took an hour for my heartbeat to return to normal. Other agents on the spot had had similar reactions and later we had a chuckle at this bad moment—and a sigh of relief that all of us had been told the facts about the Berbers before we'd had a chance to fire back at them.

On another occasion in the Middle East we received a tip that an attempt would be made on Mr. Eisenhower's life during the public festivities the next day. If this were true it would mean the cancellation of all the events planned, a difficult thing to explain to one's hosts and to the people of the country. Was our informer correct? We had only a few hours to find out before we must decide whether to proceed or to postpone everything.

That informer went through a nerve-racking grilling, I can assure you. He wouldn't admit anything for the longest time. We finally got him to break down by telling him we'd give him money if he told the truth. He gave a gap-toothed smile then and admitted he was a hoax! He only wanted Yankee dollars for his false "tip." We kept our bargain but we also saw to it that he was given some time in jail for his pains.

Perhaps the truly worst moment of all, however, was at Kabul in Afghanistan; if it were not for our presence there the President might well have died on the spot.

Kabul's altitude is some six thousand feet. This was too high for the President, as it turned out. At one point he had to walk up twenty-four steps, and when he had gotten to the top and to a reception room he fainted. Consternation reigned. An oxygen tank was required immediately.

And one was there! Right on the spot! This was due to the prescience and thoughtfulness and dedication of Dick Flohr, the President's driver and one of our really devoted Secret Service agents. Flohr hadn't liked the idea of the President walking at such altitudes. So he'd lugged the heavy oxygen equipment, which otherwise would have been on the airplane seventy miles away, around with him that day "just in case." This was thoughtfulness way beyond the call of duty.

A heart specialist later told me that Dick's preparedness probably saved the President from a serious, perhaps fatal heart attack.

President Eisenhower's travels at this juncture were all of course triumphal tours—with only one or two exceptions. The Russians hated these personal victories he was scoring and I think feared his world-wide popularity. Thus they never missed an opportunity to deprecate him, and they sometimes used the Secret Service to do so.

They tirelessly pointed out the fact that at Geneva, Khrushchev had gone around in an open car and without any guard. Whereas, they stated, Eisenhower traveled in a closed car with agents fore and aft and all around.

The fact is that nobody is as heavily guarded as Khrushchev. It is true that, on one or two occasions in Geneva, he did venture out in an open car—but this was for newspaper pictures alone. Generally he travels in a closed limousine surrounded by guards. The only conclusion I can come to about his two sallies outdoors with relatively few guards is that he's willing to risk his life for a little propaganda.

When advance Secret Service agents go to a country to prepare for our President's safety they are instructed to be unfailingly polite, never to make demands on the police of the country and always to defer to their host's wishes. Anything we want we ask for in the nicest way possible. The Russians are quite the opposite—they seem to want to chill the host's blood rather than to warm his heart.

When Khrushchev was to come here, an advance group led by a General Zakharov came over a month beforehand. Solemnly they called a meeting of our top security men. Zakharov was coldly polite to all, but then he gave his speech. "Gentlemen," he said through his interpreter, "if an attempt is made on Khrushchev's life while he is in the United States, the situation will be very very serious, even if Khrushchev doesn't die. If he does die it will be the end of the United States." Here the interpreter made a gesture with his right hand indicating the way a child might the fall of a bomb, and, as it landed he said, "Boom." Zakharov smiled bleakly. "Exactly," he said.

It was particularly appalling because nobody can absolutely guarantee the safety of any head of state. With fifty thousand potential killers among our lunatic population the United States certainly can't guarantee anybody's total safety—particularly that of Khrushchev, who can provoke perfectly sane men to murderous rage at times.

It is my opinion that Khrushchev canceled Mr. Eisenhower's trip to Russia because he feared our President's popularity. The massive good will Mr. Eisenhower was able to inspire in entire populations must have been very frightening to the Russian masters—they certainly did not wish to have any such demonstrations of affection for a "capitalist" President on their home grounds. As master strategists, therefore, they simply sidestepped the whole problem by withdrawing their invitation.

After all his success abroad I believe this was a bitter blow to Mr. Eisenhower. To him the projected journeys to Russia and Japan were to crown his peripatetic endeavors for democracy.

President Eisenhower was persuaded to continue with plans for going to Japan by Ambassador Douglas MacArthur, the General's nephew, who represented this country there. MacArthur kept sending the President reports which made one single croaking point—the President's trip was necessary if democracy was to be saved in Japan; if Mr. Eisenhower didn't come Premier Kishi's regime would fall and the extremists to the right or left would come to power. This, of course, was enormously persuasive talk.

But what I resent most about the whole inept and dangerous affair were the bland and falsely reassuring reports Mr.
MacArthur gave the advance Secret Service agents I sent over
to insure Mr. Eisenhower's safety. Oh, he said in effect to
them, pay no attention to the student riots, they don't mean
a thing. The Japanese people would not dream of harming the
person of the President. He was, of course, speaking as our
foremost expert on the matter and therefore we took him very
seriously and at his word—at first.

The very day that Japanese mobs stormed the Tokyo Parlia-
ment, wounding five hundred people, many very seriously,
MacArthur sent a cable to Mr. Eisenhower, again emphasiz-
ing how important his visit there would be and pleading that
he come. When I heard this and read of the riots on the same
day I decided to use our Ambassador to Japan as an expert no
longer. I sent word to my men to get their information from
other sources, preferably the Japanese police and military.
Very quickly then we got information that was unimpeach-
able; and it all was to the effect that if Mr. Eisenhower came
to Japan his safety could not be guaranteed, the police definitely could not control the rioters. From that moment on I
set my face firmly against the trip and, thank heavens, in the
end we on the "nay" side won the day.

The questions remain: Why did MacArthur's good sense
desert him? Why was he willing right up to the end to risk
the President's life? I can't answer those questions. I only
know that far too many men around our Presidents are quite
willing, if it will benefit them, to let the Chief Executive put
his life on the line.

The cancelation of the Japanese trip ended Mr. Eisenhower's travels for democracy and, dispiritedly, he returned home. His journeys had occupied the greater part of his second term —and had taken up a large part of my attention and energies during this time. I felt exhausted from the strain of planning and going on these magnificent but dangerous journeys, and, though I felt sorry for President Eisenhower that his term in office had to end on such an anticlimactic note, I was glad for the respite.

Nixon — An Assassin's Dreamboat

THE NIXON POLITICAL STAR LOOKED BRIGHT IN-
deed as the 1960 election drew near. I think he was, and is,
an extraordinarily fine man in all ways. But speaking entirely
as the person responsible for the President's safety, the idea
of Mr. Nixon as our Chief Executive gave me serious pause.
Viewing the utter disregard for his own personal safety which
he showed during his eight years as Vice President, I had
come to think of him as an assassin's delight, a murderer's
dreamboat. As one of my men put it after seeing him rush

toward a disorderly crowd another man would have fled from: "He has delusions of personal safety."

The same remarks might have been made of Mr. Kennedy before his election. The fact is, of course, that the two men are incorrigibly brave, utterly indifferent to their physical safety. Mr. Kennedy has settled in, however, nicely and allows the Secret Service really to protect him now that he's President. Would Mr. Nixon have done so? All I can say is that he never did so as Vice President and, indeed, on some occasions came near to being killed for this reason.

The law of the land does not *require* the Secret Service to protect the Vice President as it does the President. It states only that we are responsible for his safety if and to the degree that he asks us for our protection. Otherwise we are to keep our hands off. I consider this an outrageous law and I have personally tried to have it amended. It leaves far too much discretion in the hands of men who may be great in other ways but who don't necessarily know the least thing about when they and their families are in danger and when they're not. Such decisions can, often enough, only be made by experts.

When Mr. Nixon first came into office I had a conference with him, hoping to fill him in on the whole subject of the Secret Service and to indicate to him how much protection I thought he would need, why he'd need it and so forth. He filled me in. He said he'd only accept protection from the Secret Service when he was out of town. And only a very minimal guard even then. I felt that this was not nearly enough. Later he changed. He allowed us to assign two men to him in Washington and more when he was out of town.

As Vice President Mr. Nixon rarely departed from this basic attitude of indifference to his safety and to our efforts to protect him—though I must say he was always scrupulously polite and very appreciative of everything we did.

One of his convictions about the way he should (and should not) be guarded nearly cost him his life more than once. It was his insistence on always having his car at the head of any motorcade where he was the VIP of the day. The usual practice is to have a car of Secret Service men go first. With the President we always have a car before him and a car following immediately after.

The worst trouble Mr. Nixon's insistence caused occurred in South America. I don't think the American people fully realize how close to death Mr. Nixon and his wife came in Caracas, Venezuela. It was a blood-curdling experience, and it was entirely avoidable in the first place. I'd had a report on just how bad things were here and I didn't want the Vice President to make the trip. It was like talking into a barrel.

Mrs. Nixon accompanied her husband on this trip. After they landed at the airstrip in Caracas the plan was for them to go to the Simón Bolívar memorial by car. The mob at the airport was extremely nasty. As a prelude to what was to come they threw mud and vegetables at the American party and at the Venezuelan Consul who accompanied it. At first Mr. Nixon wanted to make the trip in an open car but, by rare good fortune, he allowed the Secret Service guard to overrule him in this single instance.

That decision almost undoubtedly saved his life and that of Mrs. Nixon.

[246]

However, though we persuaded him to go in a closed car, he still insisted that his car go first in the motorcade. Moreover, he wanted Mrs. Nixon's car to follow directly behind him. This meant that the Secret Service car had to trail two cars behind, and, as I've pointed out before, this means that we have to fight our way through the mob to get to the person we are protecting, losing valuable time and exposing him to dangers in the interim. This happened that day.

At the entrance to the city of Caracas two trucks suddenly came out of nowhere and stalled across the street the Nixon motorcade was traveling on. Immediately a mob seemed to form from nowhere, though it was clear that the whole thing had been organized. The four Secret Service agents in the car behind Mrs. Nixon immediately jumped out and tried to fight their way through the crowd. Finally and almost too late, the agents got to the Vice President's side.

But in the meantime stones pounded against the windshields and windows of both cars. The crowd, almost unopposed now, became bolder by the second. They moved in to strike the windows and side of the cars with wooden clubs, bats and pieces of iron. The car's glass was entirely pulverized. Fine particles flew through the inside of the car from the impact of the beating, cutting the occupants' faces and hands. "It was like being inside a drum," the driver said, referring to the noise of the clubs against the tonneau.

Two Secret Service men were in Mr. Nixon's car with him. Both of them agree that this mob was not just out to make anti-American propaganda. They were intent on killing Mr. Nixon. "If you had been inside that car with us," one of the agents told me, "and heard that crowd and saw their faces you would have no doubts about it. They clearly meant to get their hands on Nixon and tear him to pieces."

He was absolutely correct about that fact, for later investigation showed beyond any doubt that the mob intended to pull the Vice President from the car and stomp him to death.

The wait inside the car seemed like an eternity. Actually it was only five minutes before the Secret Service men could come abreast of the car and five more before they could clear the road.

If it had been any longer there would certainly have been at least one death. For the mob had succeeded in smashing a hole in the glass next to the Vice President and were intent on extending the breakthrough with the idea of pulling him out through it.

One remark made by Mr. Nixon stayed with me from this terrible episode. It seems to me to establish the fatalism felt by all in that entourage, to establish beyond doubt the awful seriousness of the situation. The Secret Service agent inside Mr. Nixon's car said to the Vice President after the motorcade had started to roll again: "I hope Mrs. Nixon gets through." To which Mr. Nixon replied, "If she doesn't it can't be helped." He was, at one and the same time, stating that we were doing all we possibly could and that, indeed, we were all essentially helpless in this trap we had fallen into.

The group of course completely abandoned its intention to go to the Simón Bolívar monument and, instead, took refuge in the United States Embassy. However, the very awfulness of this ordeal by autocade may have saved the lives of the Nixons. Shortly after the attack on them an empty building near the Bolívar statue was found to contain four hundred gasoline bombs, the kind called Molotov cocktails, which can be thrown by hand like grenades. It seems clear that these were intended for the Vice President and his party when they got to the monument—and thus one danger saved them from the other.

The puzzling thing about Mr. Nixon was that his experiences did not seem to temper his indiscretion. He consistently and unswervingly put principle, high policy and perhaps good politics before his personal safety. "He's far too brave for his own good," one agent told me, and that about sums it up.

Recall that during the campaign against Mr. Kennedy, Mr. Nixon ended up in the hospital with an infection of his knee. This was caused by a jostling crowd. Here is what happened.

In August of 1960 Mr. Nixon went to Greensboro, North Carolina, as part of his campaign. He gave the Secret Service specific instructions on how he wanted the crowd handled. In effect his instructions rendered our protective strategy, which included police lines and other security measures, useless. "Let them have their heads," he said in effect and, by law, we could not oppose him. Here were the results as given to me by one of my agents in a justly plaintive report:

Because of our being limited as to the number of police used, as well as physical objects to control the public (as per Mr. Nixon's advices) from the time the Vice President first appeared until he made his departure, the task of controlling the public was absolutely impossible. Apparently orderly crowds would immediately deteriorate into an ever-growing, mad, mauling melee with each individual doing his best to claw his way to some position where he hoped to be able to either touch the Vice President or speak to him. The most that those assigned to protection could possibly do was confine their efforts to trying to prevent the Vice

President and Mrs. Nixon from being crushed by the actual pressure of the mobs. It is my opinion that if such situations should continue, and should someone attempt an aggressive act against the Vice President, we could only punish and not prevent physical injury.

The man who wrote this report is ordinarily calm and imperturbable, not at all given to hysteria. Mr. Nixon, however, just shrugged the whole matter off and blithely went into another crowd that was quite as wild. During this maelstrom he was pushed or stumbled against something, perhaps a car, which injured his kneecap and it was this mishap that later landed him in the hospital.

On another occasion, when Mr. Nixon was in Chicago with his family, he specifically gave instructions that we were only to send a small Secret Service detail. He also told the Chicago police not to interfere with crowds trying to reach him. Again his attitude baffled me and I had profound misgivings about his safety. His daughters were with him on this occasion and, unhappily, my fears turned out to be justified.

Patricia and Julie, then fourteen and twelve years of age, were nearly trampled to death outside the Blackstone Hotel. A Secret Service agent with the group stated that "the crowd moved in like a juggernaut. The girls turned white with fear." Mr. Nixon was with them at the moment, and, by carefully reconstructing the event from the reports given to me by my men, I can only conclude that all three of them were very close to serious injury for several minutes.

I wish to repeat: I don't want to be misunderstood in my remarks about Mr. Nixon. In my experience all the great men I have come into contact with have been physically fearless—

it seems to be a condition of greatness. I admire the virtue profoundly. It allows such men to take action under circumstances which could paralyze other men.

This was the case when Vice President Nixon visited Pegu, Burma, at one point during his incumbency. His party had arrived in the village of Pegu through a narrow corridor of land surrounded by Communist guerrillas. In the center of this town an English-speaking demagogue with a sound truck had whipped up a crowd of listeners into an anti-American fury.

The Burmese police didn't like the looks of things at all. And neither did the Secret Service guard I had sent along. Nixon was, however, totally unperturbed. He sized up the situation and, telling his entire security force to stay behind, he went right over to the man on the sound truck and struck up a conversation with him.

"As he talked to the man," one of my agents said, "the anti-American banners they were holding started to go down. As he continued to talk, the mood of the crowd changed to a much friendlier tone." In the end he had made a group of dangerous enemies into friends.

When bravery can have such results in this day and age of perpetual crisis it may be worth the candle after all. Perhaps Mr. Nixon will yet have a chance to show his mettle and his qualities in the Presidency itself. I wish him well in such a case, and the Chief who succeeds me I wish well too, should he ever have to assume full responsibility for the protection of this aggressively fearless man and his lovely family.

chapter 19

My Last President

I COME NOW TO THE LAST CHAPTER; THE END OF the Eisenhower regime and the safe launching of the Kennedys into the ways of life in the White House. I opened this account with my very great disturbance when I saw the smoke rising from the lectern as Cardinal Cushing rendered the invocation at President-Elect Kennedy's Inaugural. I realized that night as I went from one festivity to another checking on our elaborate security preparations that I was tired, very, very tired.

I had noticed this unusual tiredness before; after the last great journey Mr. Eisenhower took to the Far East. The tension and fatigue I felt after this trip had been very persistent;

they hung on and on and at my wife's insistence I even went to see the doctor. He wanted to know how long I'd been with the Secret Service and I told him over thirty-three years. He said, "That's too long to be in the saddle," and I agreed with him—in principle. However, I shrugged off the implications. Besides I really found the challenge of this fresh, new, handsome couple and their enchanting family very stimulating and, for a while, the new regime made me forget my weariness.

Packing off the retiring incumbents of the White House and getting the newcomers settled in is a very confusing job—particularly since, despite our long preparations for it, the final act of moving out and the process of moving in takes place on the same day—Inauguration Day.

I paid my final respects to President and Mrs. Eisenhower and they were very kind in the things they said to me personally, and in the things they said about the job we had done for them. They left that afternoon for Gettysburg and I was able to forget my natural sadness at seeing them go by turning my full attention to my new charges.

The White House, as the Kennedys moved in that afternoon, was one large seething mass of hustle and another large seething mass of bustle. Groups of people were all over the place. These were not strangers, though their faces were new to the White House Police and the permanent White House staff.

Many of them were Kennedys. There are well over fifty in the family. Still others were friends of the family. And there were, also, new members of the government, Cabinet officials, *et al*. And also there were the Kennedys' servants, some of whom they had brought with them. What with people carrying and fetching, or just standing around having a good time looking happy, pandemonium, albeit a gay one, reigned.

The presence of these new and largely unfamiliar faces on the first day of the new regime in the White House always creates a definite security problem. The White House Police and the White House Detail can't, of course, accost everybody and ask them who they are and please to prove it; they may be insulting the President's father or the new Secretary of the Interior by such fatuous inquiries. Yet we have to know who's who, for at this juncture an assassin could very easily join the festivities unaccosted.

Thus, weeks, and even months, beforehand, we start collecting pictures of a new President's family, friends and appointees. Bob Bouck of Protective Research was in charge of this detail, which we called Operation Snapshot. We got pictures of the newcomers from *Life* Magazine, *Newsweek* and *Time;* we searched newspaper morgues; we called relatives and asked them for anything they could spare from their albums. Wherever we could get the proper snapshots we got them, scores of them. And then, when we had enough, we made our own album and had the Secret Service agents and the White House Police study the faces in it until they could match names with physiognomies in a flash. So successful was Operation Snapshot that not a single relative, close friend or appointee received any unnecessary challenge despite the confusion of this exciting day.

The public seemed truly delighted at Mr. Kennedy's election and the White House mail increased enormously. Until Kennedy's election Mr. Eisenhower's first six weeks in office held the record for the volume of mail received by any President. For the same period Mr. Kennedy's mail ran over 50 per cent greater.

On the dark side, the number of letters from the lunatic fringe increased by 300 per cent! And there was also a great increase in the number of insane people who tried to phone the President or who stopped at the White House gates to threaten his life and the lives of members of his family.

There were of course many letters from religious fanatics. Typical was one from Los Angeles which read: "We are sick of the dirty black Catholics. . . . The next bomb will be for you Mr. Kennedy." And another which read: "With a completely divided America there is speculation about your safety . . . they will never support you. . . . You must surely know that you are no more fit to be President than my tomcat—or are you so stupid and arrogant that you don't even know that much?"

There was of course the usual "You can send me $500 or I'll kill you on sight." And a missive that wandered all over the place till it came to its mad conclusion: "We are talking of assassination plans—not just Jack but old Red-headed peppery Joe and little baby brother Bobbie."

We paid very much attention to them, as always (recall Pavlick), and many of the senders and callers ended up in institutions, some for life. One inexplicable change in the tenor of these letters: while they remained as threatening as ever there were far fewer obscenities in them. For that much, at any rate, we could be thankful.

There was also a tremendous increase in the number of

presents sent to the President. By the end of February, 1961, after six weeks in office, Mr. and Mrs. Kennedy had received over ten thousand gifts from all parts of the United States.

However, the President refused to accept a large part of the gifts sent, laying down a new policy for the White House. Mr. Kennedy and his First Lady send back many of the costly and even some of the less expensive ones. I felt this was a very thoughtful and sensitive policy to establish.

The new couple in the White House are, in fact, very sensitive and thoughtful people altogether. I was soon struck by Mr. Kennedy's almost awesome egalitarianism in public, in some ways even greater than Mr. Truman's. As my wife put it after meeting him on one occasion: "Whoever he's with, he's with them completely."

This is absolutely so, whether the person is a little Girl Scout there to present him with a plaque, one of his gardeners or a member of his Cabinet. One knows at once in his presence that he is thoroughly aware of you and really cares about what makes you tick. And he does.

As a brief proof of this point: On one of his daily visits to his wife during her stay at Georgetown Hospital, which is largely staffed by nuns, one of the older Sisters got up her courage and asked him with obvious trepidation if she might take his picture. He said of course she could and stood still for her to do so. She had a large vintage Brownie Kodak, a tenacious survivor from another time, and she pointed it at him. But she was dreadfully nervous at this proximity to the first Catholic to become a President and her hands shooks so badly that she couldn't take the picture. The President tried to calm her by saying he'd take one of her afterward but she was unable to stop her quivering. Finally another nun, almost as old as she was, said, "Here, I'll do it," and bravely took the camera. She too, however, was suddenly stricken by stage fright and her hands also started to shake. The President, at length, in the softest and most reassuring of voices said, "That's all right. I'll be back tomorrow and you can take one then." He was back too; their shock at their boldness had died down and the picture was taken without a tremor to speak of.

I met Mrs. Kennedy for the first time at Georgetown Hospital when I went there to check on our security arrangements for her lying-in. She was absolutely charming. She was also absolutely clear about what her relationship and that of her family would be with the Secret Service. From the first she had not wanted Caroline, and of course later John, Jr., to become dependent on the Secret Service or overly attached to any given agent. I profoundly respected these sentiments and was able to assure her that we could easily prevent such eventualities. My security plans for Caroline and her little brother therefore were made with Mrs. Kennedy's desires very much in mind.

The First Lady's looks and artistic abilities have been covered in reams of newspaper and magazine copy. I have not seen, however, very much said about a far more important virtue to my way of thinking—her relationship with her children and her attitude toward being a mother.

From all I could see or hear she is one of the finest mothers I have ever known—despite the very real difficulties a President's wife has in such a role. With all the other demands on her she sees to it that John, Jr. and Caroline are along with her whenever she can possibly have them—and she sees to it that that's frequently.

When she takes her brood along she piles Caroline into the front seat of her blue Pontiac station wagon, has the collapsible baby carriage put in back, sets little John up in his bassinet and off she goes, herself at the wheel, like any other young suburban mother. She takes them perhaps to a park in the Georgetown area where she knows many other young mothers, or off to visit a friend with a little girl Caroline's age. We don't ride in the station wagon with her, in deference to her wishes. The Secret Service tags along behind at a discreet distance in another car, and the agents call in to my office on their shortwave sets exactly where they are at any given time.

The things Mrs. Kennedy says about being a mother and also about being a wife strike me as more than memorable. So strongly have they impressed me that I've collected some of them. Here are a few:

"If you bungle raising your children, I don't think whatever else you do will matter much."

"My greatest joy is just being with my children."

"I never want a home where you have to say to children, 'Don't touch.'"

"The most important thing for a successful marriage is for the husband to do what he likes best and does well. The wife's satisfactions will follow."

"Happiness is not where you think you find it. I'm determined not to worry. So many people poison every day worrying about the next."

To me such statements indicate that we have a truly remarkable person as our First Lady. I have a strong feeling, having had a closer view than most, that she will be one of the great Presidents' wives in our history.

The youth, energy and physical prowess of the Kennedys caused a tremendous amount of speculation about the security problems they would create for the Secret Service. I was phoned constantly and asked whether my men would be able to keep up with the new President's pace.

We were spared no single jibe. Did we have a Weissmuller to go along with the President on swimming jaunts—Mr. Kennedy had been a member of the Harvard swimming team, hadn't he? The President was an expert handler of small sailing craft; were we giving the White House Detail lessons in seamanship? And what about Mrs. Kennedy's fox hunting? Would we follow her on foot? Were we thinking of putting some gentleman riders on the White House Detail?

All these problems the reporters asked about were basically real ones. However, solutions to them, while they had to be sought, were relatively easy to find.

When the President is in swimming it is a simple matter to have a rowboat ready in case of an emergency no matter what his natatory prowess may be. I think our agents would be able to row faster than even President Kennedy can swim.

And as for fox hunting, many of the members of the Secret Service ride at least as well as the top hunt members. Some of our men, for one example, were recruited from state police departments. These organizations often teach their men, routinely, to ride standing on two horses and to jump through burning hoops. I do not think they'll be required to jump through burning hoops while riding to hounds. Also, these men regularly ride across far rougher country with higher and tougher jumps than one finds in the fox hunting area of Virginia. Some of my men are such excellent riders that their chief problem may well be in disguising their proficiency from less well-seated members of the hunting set—as a matter of diplomacy of course.

The President's love of small sailing craft, too, can easily be handled as a security problem. A high-powered motorboat standing far enough from him not to interfere with his privacy or fun could still get to him in seconds if any trouble should develop. Indeed, this kind of protection was the same as we finally worked out for Mr. Truman on his walks: the high-powered automobile with rifles and riot guns which lurked far behind but which always kept him in view.

I've mentioned before that each President and his family present unique security problems. These spring from the individuals, their temperaments, their personalities, their good or bad health: Mr. Eisenhower's physical restlessness and his illnesses, Mr. Truman's irrepressible energy and friendliness, Margaret Truman's career-mindedness. The Kennedys are no exception. However, the chief security problem we've had to solve for them has not sprung from their youthful exuberance, as most people felt it would, but from a really odd and unexpected source—their exquisite taste.

There is no question in my mind but that the place the President and First Lady selected for themselves at Middleburg, Virginia, is, artistically speaking, an absolute jewel. The house is situated on four hundred acres of the most beautiful countryside I have ever seen, in the very heart of the fox hunting region. It and the grounds around it are indescribably lovely; and Mrs. Kennedy's décor has made the house a pleasure dome, at least for the eye. Once the Kennedys had seen the whole layout they fell in love with it and no consideration could have weighed in the balance against their enthusiasm.

I was silent on the matter for that reason—it would have been unavailing to speak. The fact is, however, that from the standpoint of protecting the family, there is one serious drawback in Middleburg. It is that there is only one road that leads to the estate from the highway; and, what is worse, it is only wide enough for one car to go over in one direction at a time. If cars should meet while on it one must back up.

Solving the problem of making Middleburg safe for the President was not easy, as you can see.

The final solution was threefold. To get as much mobility as possible we had a special heliport constructed and a helicopter kept in constant readiness when the President or his family was present.

Also, we made all possible arrangements to keep the single road to the house open at all times. To do this we installed a short-wave system. This linked an agent at the entrance of the road to our central post on the grounds. Thus we knew what was on the road to and from the house at any moment and could close it off to all traffic in one second flat.

But the basic part of my plan was to make the grounds virtually impregnable to an invasion by troublemakers. To that end we had four guardhouses put in at strategic points. (Recall, only two were thought necessary at Gettysburg.) Also, I had a central command post set up in two trailers which contains every form of communication, from a PA system which can bawl out instructions in a tremendous voice that would reach all the guardhouses in case of an emergency, to microwave and short-wave radio systems and teletype and telephonic

[261]

communications. If we were ever in any danger which the Secret Service could not manage with the men it had, the local police, Virginia State Police and the Washington Metropolitan Police (Middleburg is only forty-odd miles from the District of Columbia) as well as the United States Army and Air Force could be notified in one second and be there in the next.

However, I don't think we'll ever have to call for help, short of a foreign invasion. I've had a regular arsenal installed at Middleburg, from tear gas bombs to every conceivable kind of gun—machine guns, skat guns, carbines, armor-piercing rifles, etc.

With such preparations, then, I tried to make up for the inherent deficiency (poor mobility) forced on us by the location, by being on a constant alert for all kinds of emergencies and by being virtually impregnable to attack.

I quoted Mrs. Kennedy earlier as saying that if you mess up your children's upbringing nothing else you do will matter too much one way or the other. It's too early to say anything about John, Jr. of course but the Secret Service can speak out loudly and clearly about Caroline. Mrs. Kennedy has certainly not bungled the job with her. She is utterly delightful and spontaneous, affectionate, curious, all the things that a wonderful little girl can be.

John, Jr. and Caroline are, of course, the first small children of a Presidential couple since Teddy Roosevelt lived in the White House. I must say that, as in the most ordinary house, children add a great deal to the feeling of pleasurable hominess in the stately and historic old manse.

The protection of children is a very special and sensitive

mission, as we saw in the case of President Eisenhower's grandchildren. The Kennedys specified that they did not want their boy and girl to become too dependent on the Secret Service or too attached to any one agent.

This meant I had to select men for Caroline's detail who were particularly good with children and sensitive to their needs and yet it also meant that I had to change them often enough to prevent the little girl from getting too attached to any one of them.

To keep Caroline from becoming dependent on them I instructed the men to stay as far away from her as possible. With a child particularly, out of sight means out of mind.

Caroline, however, is as bright as a new dollar and she knew from the beginning the agents following her were in her party. "Hurry up, slowpoke," she would call after them as they ambled after her and her nurse at Palm Beach. On one occasion she threatened one of her men, "If you don't catch up with us we're going to leave you." Finally we decided to tell her that the agents were friends who liked to come along with her. She accepted that idea readily.

Caroline looks very much like her father and is generally recognized in public because of this resemblance to him. She is quite a chatterbox (or, as one agent put it in a routine report to me, "a good conversationalist") and loves to talk to everybody and anybody. She has an excellent memory and learns the name of every agent on her detail after hearing it only once. On New Year's Day one of the agents, who had been introduced to her only once three days previously, was as surprised as pleased to have her say to him when she saw him: "Happy New Year, Mr. Tucker."

She loves to play with other children and does it very well. She will talk to them endlessly, asking them all sorts of questions about their mothers and fathers and brothers and sisters. She is very attached to her own baby brother and she states very clearly that his name is John, not Jack. When people ask her (as I inadvertently did) how her brother Jack is, she always says: "It's not Jack, it's John. Jack is my father's name."

I could tell many stories about Caroline's gaiety and charm; but I shall leave that to the newspapers, who find Caroline an inexhaustible source of such tales. It is enough to know that I made my contribution to the plans for protecting this little girl and her wonderful family before I retired as Chief of the Secret Service.

As I prepared the future security of the new President and his family and engaged in the other manifold work of the Secret Service, time again began to slip away on me. Fall passed into winter and, when I looked up, there was one more spring in Washington.

I well remember one particular day of that lovely spring. It was an incredibly beautiful day in May. I drove to work through a world of beginnings, for everywhere everything had broken into blossom and bloom. I suddenly didn't feel my too familiar weariness any more. But somehow I didn't want to go to my office. I did go, however, through years of accumulated habit, and when I got there I felt intolerably restless; cabined and confined, imprisoned.

My wife had been after me to retire again—just the night before. Her arguments were good, irrefutable. I'd done my job. I needed change, to loaf and to invite my soul. I'd earned it. She said all this but somehow I had hardly listened to her. However, now, suddenly, her words became meaningful. There was no real problem. I was eligible to retire, eminently so. I had put in thirty-three years of service and was five years over the retirement age.

I looked out the window of the Treasury Building at the blue spring skies, at the visitors to Washington strolling on Pennsylvania Avenue. You could tell the visitors from the workers by their leisurely gait, and their air of relaxed enjoyment. I had never walked like that in Washington; I had always walked like a worker, harassed, full of duties and responsibilities. . . .

I paced around my office. My wall was hung with pictures of the people I had known and the people I had protected; and, too, on the walls were twelve separate awards I'd been given since becoming Chief thirteen years before. Odd—thirteen years as the thirteenth Chief of the Secret Service. I stopped before one of the awards now, a citation from the American Veterans of World War II. The words were like those in the other eleven. "In recognition of outstanding public service." I'd never really read the citation itself before, that is, not with attention. I did now. It said, in part:

Mr. Baughman has been singularly successful as head of the Secret Service because he combines an exceptional background in technical enforcement work with an intelligent understanding of the administrative problems of his organization. During the past several years, the world-wide travels of both the President and Vice President have tested the ability of the Secret Service to fulfill its role of guaranteeing the well-being of both men under the most arduous conditions. That the Secret Service carried out its mission with complete and total success is a tribute in the highest form to training programs and policies introduced into the service by Chief Baughman.

The citation went on and on and, while it was on the rhetorical side, it moved me curiously. I gave a deep sigh, I recall, after I'd finished it. What it said was that I'd done my job, done it for a long time and done it well. For the first time I thought: "Perhaps that's true; perhaps I've done enough. Perhaps I ought to relax now and let others take over."

I took up my hat on a sudden impulse and left the office without telling anybody where I was going. It was the first time, too, that I'd done that in over thirty-three years of work. But somehow I felt they'd get along without me, an entirely new idea in my psychology. On the wave of my new feeling I walked around Washington for hours, looking at things I'd always wanted to, but mainly just letting the feeling of leisure penetrate my being. I stayed out till 3:30 P.M. and on my way back I called my wife and told her we were going to retire. She was beside herself with joy. "Have you told them already?" she asked, as if fearful that I'd back down on my decision.

"Yes," I lied.

But I made good on that white lie at once. I went back and phoned Secretary of the Treasury Dillon to tell him of my decision. Saying good-by to a lifetime of work was as easy as that; a simple phone call and your whole life could be changed!

Set in Fairfield
Format by Séamus Byrne
Manufactured by The Haddon Craftsmen, Inc.
Published by HARPER & BROTHERS, New York